Jason Ingram

Edited by Beverly Banks
Copyright © 2016 Accelerated Wealth

Accelerated Wealth
13570 Meadowgrass Drive
Suite 200
Colorado Springs, CO 80921

ISBN: 978-1-5399865-6-0

United States of America

Accelerated Wealth

Real Financial Planning
for Today's Economy

By Jason Ingram

Table of Contents

Section I: How Did We Get Here?

Section II: 4 D's to
        Accelerated Wealth

9-11-15

MICHAEL...
Good luck + to Your Life

Section III: The Second D: The Diagnostic Phase

Section IV: The Design Phase

Section V: The 4th D: The Delivery

Dedication

To my late dear mother, Alma Mae, whose guidance and belief in me and my abilities never faltered, even once. She was truly the personification of Agape Love. In the darkest hours and when I feared I might not succeed, she was there with the greatest encouragement of all, "If anyone can do it, you can." She is the gazelle in the Lion and the Gazelle story. That short verse was on the wall of her sewing room and she knew absolutely that when the sun comes up, you'd better be running.

We're doin' it, Alma!!

Foreword

**BY ACCELERATED WEALTH FOUNDER and
CEO BILL WALTON**

Over the last twenty-three years, I have been involved with both adults and youth in business as an entrepreneur and in ministry as a pastor. I have had success in both endeavors. A common thread has run through my experiences: people seek the truth and transparency. They look for solutions that fit their lives and make sense.

As a contractor, I felt the excitement that comes with success and growth. I have worried about payroll and margins. I have paid taxes and tried to provide my employees with the best benefits. I have felt the frustration in seeing my hard-earned profits go more and more for taxes, and the helplessness of little or no control over how my government spends. I have seen the national debt rise, and heard the promises made by politicians in both parties to make it better. I have experienced the gridlock that characterizes our present day representatives. I knew there was something I could do that would make the climb to success easier and more attainable for the average small business owner. I knew there were financial planning answers that would address some of the fears and the anxiety so many face upon retirement.

As a minister, I have felt the burden of bad decisions people had made in personal and financial life. I have seen the destruction of debt and the heartbreak of an unsecure future. I have felt the burden that adults feel when they have to depend upon the state or their children to support them as they age. I have seen the expense of long-term care and the impact it has on a family spiritually and financially. I have seen corrections in the market ruin a family's plan for retirement. I knew there must be something I could do to help beyond my words and prayers.

My experiences became the seeds for Accelerated Wealth, which were planted and nurtured seven years ago. I had a vision that by utilizing some of the best minds and experts we could truly make a difference in the individual and the small business owner's life. We began to address the issues of taxes, losses and fees in the market, and interests paid on purchases. We began to see there was a better question to ask a client than, "What is your risk tolerance?" We began formulating the foundation for what has now become the Accelerated Wealth Strategy. We met with thousands of people. Many were just beginning their financial lives. Others were nearing retirement and weren't sure if and when they could retire. Some had retired but were concerned they did not have a plan to ensure they didn't run out of money before they ran out of life. I listened as children told me stories of how their parents had become ill, and the expense of long-term care for parents that now rested on their shoulders. I listened as others shared with me how in a few short months they had seen the nest egg they built over 30 years lose 50% of its value. They confided in me the difficulty of having to go back to work after they thought they had retired and would play golf or be with their grandchildren. I watched and listened as they confessed to me the helplessness they felt about their financial future even though they had done "everything right."

By putting some of the best minds in the country to work on solutions addressing those fundamental human and financial issues, we have created a unique way to look at and make financial plans, regardless of your age or success. By utilizing a process, we call the 4 D's (Discovery, Diagnosis, Design & Delivery), * we are able to communicate and collaborate WITH our client to find a wealth strategy that fits his or her Life Stage and truly addresses the Retirement Killers (Taxes, Loss of Spouse – Pension Rescue, Inflation, Long-Term Care, Longevity – Outliving our Income, Losses and Fees in the Market) and other issues and concerns we all face.

We have been featured on Fox News and Fox Business, as well as in Forbes Magazine and other publications. This book is written to assist you if you are nearing retirement, if you are in it already, or if you wonder whether you will ever be able to retire. We know our strategies work because they have been proven. We have thousands of clients who no longer run to the mailbox dreading that quarterly statement. We see the needs of others as opportunity. Our clients sleep at night. Our wish for you is that we might in some small way contribute to your peace of mind and allow you to be able to help others do the same. This is our mission and it begins with you.

We started in Colorado and are now in five states with thirteen offices. Our growth is real because we care about you. We want to know what keeps you up at night and what fuels your dreams!

Bill Walton
Founder and CEO of Accelerated Wealth Advisors®

Our mission is to empower our clients to achieve long-term financial health by partnering with and educating them on safe, secure and proven financial strategies.

The Heart of Accelerated Wealth Advisors:
The Lion and the Gazelle – Jason Ingram

Every morning in Africa, a gazelle wakes up. It knows it must run faster than the fastest lion or it will be eaten. Every morning a lion wakes up. It knows it must outrun the slowest gazelle or it will starve to death. It doesn't matter whether you are a lion or a gazelle . . . when the sun comes up, you'd better be running!

The analogy of the gazelle and the lion mirrors the modern day world of finance, especially retirement planning. The Employee Benefit Research Institute, a non-profit research group based in Washington, D.C., found that a third of middle income workers will likely run out of money after 20 years of retirement. The news gets worse with each generation, with Baby Boomers and Generation X future retirees having a 45% to 47% chance of being unlikely to have enough money for basic retirement costs and uninsured medical expenses.

The moral of the story: there are a lot of gazelles for the lions to feast upon. The greatest fear of most people is neither death nor public speaking, it is outliving their money. The good news, it doesn't have to be this way!

As one of the first advisors for Accelerated Wealth Advisors®, I have actively participated in creating our concepts of sensible financial solutions, eagerly watching as they have been recognized and our operations have grown beyond our original two offices. We now have thirteen offices in five states, and we have been featured in Fox Business, Forbes Magazine and on Fox Business Financial. Why? We offer both individuals and businesses a sensible plan for their retirement and a way to help insulate them from the tremendous swings in the market. We offer a plan based not on theory or hope, but on safe, proven and predictable strategies. We are not financial planners, we are **wealth strategists**. We seek to create long-term financial health for our clients. The many clients we have can attest to the fact that our plan works!

Our philosophy is simple. As a wealth strategy firm, we don't believe in a "one size fits all" financial strategy. We come alongside our clients and help them identify areas where they are UNKNOWINGLY and UNNECESSARILY transferring their hard earned wealth to others, and then we incorporate time-tested and trusted strategies to ACCELERATE the realization of their dreams and goals, whether in the business environment or in their family. At Accelerated Wealth Advisors®, we don't rush to sell products. Instead, our focus is on the "story" of each individual client. We seek to understand issues and concerns that keep our clients up at night, as well as the dreams that keep them fueled. We believe that by understanding and listening first, together we can build a financial strategy that can withstand lifestyle changes, economic volatility, and government policy change. Our goal is pretty simple: to ensure that 100% of our clients are in a significantly better financial position after meeting us than they were when walking through our doors for the first time. We see ourselves as puzzle masters. Our passion is assisting those we meet to see how that jigsaw puzzle fits together and becomes a beautiful painting. Helping others reach their financial goals is the fuel that keeps us going every time we meet a new family or business owner.

The Greek language is rich with meaning far beyond the English language. For instance, the word "Time" has two different meanings in Greek. The word *kairos* is an ancient Greek word meaning "opportunity," "season," or "fitting time." Another Greek word for "time" is *chronos*. A sequence of moments was expressed as *chronos*, emphasizing the duration of the time; an appointed time was expressed as *kairos*, with no regard for the length of the time. Thus, *chronos* was more linear and quantitative, and *kairos* was more nonlinear and qualitative.

Chronos is man's time. When the physician tells a young couple that their new baby will be born on January 31st that is chronos or man's time. When the father rushes the new mom to the hospital on the 28th that is kairos, or God's time. He didn't respond to his wife's insistence that it was time, saying, "No honey, the doctor said the baby is coming on the 31st." He rushed to the hospital and the baby was born soon after.

This is truly the story of God's time – Kairos. With so many retiring and looking to retirement, it is the season, it is the fitting time, it is the time for the opportunity, to find a better way to plan and retire. We are on a mission to help people truly understand their finances with no mumbo-jumbo or computer programs spitting out a plan. For you this book is written with love – another word that has meanings in Greek that are so much more vibrant than they are in English. I share with you the Accelerated Wealth Advisors retirement strategies with Agape love – love expecting nothing in return – but that you find peace and security in your work and retirement.

How well do you sleep at night?

It's 2:00 A.M. You're exhausted but your mind won't quit
 racing. You toss and turn. You can't get any sleep, so you get up and check your bank statement on the computer…again. For most of us it's money that's keeping us awake at night. The prospect of paying for college. Worrying if you're going to lose money if the market drops again. Wondering if you'll have to work forever because you don't have enough saved up for retirement.

At 2 A.M., you don't know where to turn for guidance. All you want is for that wheel to stop turning as you lie awake. You need a sounding board, a trusted guide. And most importantly someone to ask the right questions to cut through the non-stop static in your head – somebody to help you create a concrete action plan.

Section I:
How Did We Get Here?

Chapter 1

The U.S. Economic Forecast

Does it seem like the U.S. Government plays by a different set of accounting rules? There is a reason for this – they do. Congress has the ability to legitimize their accounting systems and practices through legislation. If any of us tried to run our individual finances or business using the accounting system the government uses, we would be in prison for financial fraud and tax evasion. Congress and the U.S. Government are above the laws which they have mandated for the rest of us. For an individual or business, if you max out your existing lines of credit, you have to convince your banker you are credit worthy to gain additional financing. Congress just has to pass legislation to increase the debt ceiling. If the rest of us were allowed to operate this way, chaos would rule!

A Brief History of the Economic Hurricane of 2000 to 2010

A series of events starting with the bursting of the tech bubble has helped unleash an economic hurricane. During 1999 and early 2000, the U.S. Federal Reserve increased interest rates six times. On March 10, 2000, the technology- heavy NASDAQ Composite index peaked at 5,048.62. This was more than double its value just a year before. On April 4, 2001, the NASDAQ fell from 4,283 points to 3,649 and rebounded back to 4,223. At the time, this represented the most volatile day in the history of the NASDAQ. Most of the tech startups had burned through their venture capital and were unable to borrow at the increased rates. By early 2001, the tech bubble had completely deflated.

Later that year, the terrorist attacks of September 11, 2001, brought chaos to the U.S. markets. Stocks plummeted. The government closed the markets to stave off more panic trading. When the markets reopened, investor confidence was clearly gone. Fueled by sub-prime lending practices, the next financial crisis was the Great Recession. According to the U.S. National Bureau of Economic Research (the official arbiter of U.S. recessions) the recession began in December 2007 and ended in June 2009, lasting over 18 months.

Part of this volatility was caused by flash trading. Flash trading is a controversial computerized trading practice offered by some market centers. Flash trading uses highly sophisticated high-speed computer technology to allow traders to view orders from other market participant's fractions of a second before others in the marketplace. This gives flash traders the advantage of being able to gauge supply and demand and recognize movements in market sentiment before other traders.

America suffered another mini-economic crisis on May 6, 2010. This has become known as The May 6, 2010 Flash Crash, aka The Crash of 2:45. During this Flash Crash, the Dow Jones Industrial Average plunged about 1000 points (about 9%) only to recover those losses within minutes. It was the second largest point swing, 1,010.14 points, and the biggest one-day point decline, 998.5 points, on an intra-day basis in Dow Jones Industrial Average history.

The Perfect Storm

The current economic storm in which our country is caught has many contributing factors. Trying to untangle this ball of yarn is like an economic game of the chicken and the egg. At the end of 2013, unemployment stood at 6.7 percent. This figure is deceptively low because it does not reflect the millions of Americans whose benefits have run out or who are grossly underemployed. The national debt – aka the federal debt – is the total of all the past years' budget deficits, minus what the government has paid off with budget surpluses. Currently this figure stands $19.27 trillion dollars and is rising every second. See National Debt Clock - http://www.usdebtclock.org.

Add to the unemployment rate and the national debt a taxing system that is completely incomprehensible to most individuals not holding an accounting degree and to a few that do. Taxpayers in the highest tax bracket – earning more than $400,000 as single filers or $450,000 filing jointly – saw their federal income tax rate increase from 35% to 39.6%. This is a significant increase, but much less than what the White House had asked Congress to pass. While the top 1% of taxpayers will bear the biggest burden, many other families, affluent as well as poor, will pay more also. While new taxes are never good news for taxpayers, we can at least be thankful that it's not worse. So where are tax rates likely to be now that the American Taxpayer Relief Act of 2012 has become law?

Potential Tax Rate Changes
2012 and 2013 maximum federal tax rates under current law

Another contributing factor to the economic storm is the personal debt load of Americans. The average American household with at least one credit card had nearly $15,756 in credit card debt in 2016 according to CreditCards.com. The average interest rate runs in the mid to high teens at any given time. In addition, Americans have a massive amount of student loan debt. Seven out of ten college seniors (71%) who graduated last year have student loan debt. In 2015 the average graduate had $35,000 in student loans. According to *Market Watch* in a January 2016 article, student loan debts grows at $2,726 per second. Many graduates are unable to find jobs that allow them to service the loans.

Inflation and the rising cost of healthcare add velocity to the storm. I like to teach my clients about inflation by telling them that their last car will cost more than their first house. The typical retired person or person nearing retirement will usually say they spent between $10,000 to $12,000 to purchase their first home. I then ask them to think about how much they paid for their last car. That's a good example of inflation.

Inflation Checklist				
	Single-Family Home	A Loaf of Bread	College Education Cost Per Year	Gallon of Unleaded Gas
	+68%	+97%	+214%	+193%
1991	$97,100	$0.72	$5,452	$1.12
2001	$147,800	$1.01	$9,032	$1.13
2011	$163,500	$1.42	$17,131	$3.28

Where is the economic train wreck heading?
The short answer – you must release your income, pension, and financing from these volatile systems and be as self-reliant as possible. You and your legacy must become self-sufficient.

Chapter 2

To Move Forward You Have to Take a Look Back: Outdated Financial Plans from the 1950's

Here is what you may have encountered: You walk into a traditional financial planner's or broker/dealer's office. After the usual exchange of small talk, the first question is, "So, what's your risk tolerance?" You are asked to fill out a form designed to rate your risk tolerance. Translated, this question and form really mean, "How much are you willing to lose?"

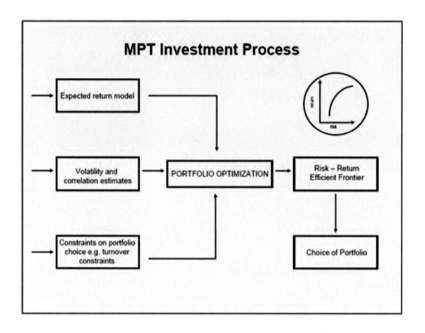

By today's standards, this question dates back to an ancient and outdated investment strategy called The Modern Theory of Portfolio Management. The theory was developed in the 1950's and became commonplace by the 1960's. Modern Portfolio Theory (MPT), also known as Portfolio Theory, was introduced by **Harry Markowitz** in his paper "Portfolio Selection," which appeared in the 1952 Journal of Finance. He won the 1990 Nobel Memorial Prize in Economic Sciences for this work. The idea was to diversify one's portfolio with different market sectors that were not completely or positively correlated. A portfolio would be divided up among large capital, mid-cap, small-cap, international and bond funds. If you were on the aggressive side, you would have fewer bonds and more equities and possibly more international funds. If your risk tolerance was rated as more conservative, you would have a higher percentage of bond funds. The use of modern portfolio theory leads to one-size-fits all financial planning strategies. When it comes to personal wealth management, one size definitely does not fit all!

We all have different needs, dreams, and plans for the future.

This portfolio was then, and still is, typically displayed as a pie chart on many financial statements. This strategy tended to work very well in helping people protect and grow their wealth especially during the four-decade run from 1960 to March of 2000. But in early 2000 the first major crack in this strategy revealed itself in a big way with the bursting of the tech bubble and the terrorist attacks on 9/11/2001. The market dropped in double digits for 3 years in a row, and the diversified pie chart portfolio crashed with losses up to 50%. We saw the failure of this strategy again in 2008-2009 when some portfolios lost up to 50% in a matter of 7 months. What amazes me is that after 12 years, in a globally connected world where 70 percent of the market is driven by computer trading known as flash trading, most financial advisors as well as individuals in retirement or approaching retirement are still using this failed strategy in the attempt to manage risk and provide lifetime income through retirement. This has led to complete portfolio disconnect. Portfolio disconnect occurs when you think your nest egg that you have worked so long to build is in a safe position with minimal risk. After an analysis is complete, it shows it may all be at risk.

While there used to be an inverse relationship between stocks and bonds, that all changed in the 2001-2002 correction and during the 2007-08 recession. In the past when stocks went down, bonds would balance the portfolio. Bonds were the safe haven. Not any longer, during both of those 'corrections' bonds were subject to Market Value Adjustment, Interest Rate Risk, Inflation Risk, Call Risk and in the case of foreign bonds, Currency Risks. Bonds went down in value just like the rest of the portfolio they were supposed to protect.

The only inverse relationship with bonds in these financial times are interest rates. When interest rates go up bonds go down in value and vice-versa. Bonds are no longer the safe- haven; yet most financial salespersons continue to utilize these in your portfolio. Depending on your age, you may have as much as an 80/20 split between bonds and securities. While this may fit the suitability standard of the broker/dealer salesman, it certainly may not be in your best interest. This can be a scenario for disaster.

Stocks and bonds have a limited amount of diversification

possibilities. Even though most financial advisors call it diversification, stocks and bonds tend to trend together. Additionally, when interest rates are low, corporations have the opportunity to do debt market value adjustments, which can impact the value of corporate bonds.

Well-known critics of MPT include Nassim Nicholas Taleb (author of *The Black Swan*) and Ray Dalio, CEO of Bridgewater Associates, one of the largest hedge funds in the world with roughly $80 billion in assets under management. The very foundation of modern asset allocation just doesn't work, they say.

According to the findings of Pricewaterhouse Coopers (PwC) — the largest professional services firm in the world and one of the Big Four auditors along with Deloitte, EY and KPMG — this adds to concerns raised earlier about the viability of the 4 percent rule.

Research published in 2013 by Michael Finke of Texas Tech University, Wade Pfau of the American College, and David Blanchett of Morningstar Investment Management found that using historical interest rate averages, a retiree drawing down savings for a 30-year retirement using the 4 percent rule had only a 6 percent chance of running out. But using interest rate levels from January 2013, when their research was published, the authors found that the savings of retirees would grow so slowly that the chance of failure rose to 57 percent.

"The 4 percent rule cannot be treated as a safe initial withdrawal rate in today's low interest rate environment," they concluded.

According to the Wall Street Journal, plans utilizing Modern Portfolio Management theory with a 4% drawdown have a 57% failure rate. Think of it this way. You just got on an airplane. The captain makes his normal preflight greeting. "It is sunny and warm at our destination today. Our flight has a 43% chance of arriving." Do you stay on the plane? NO! You look for a better airline with better equipment and a team that is highly trained to make sure you make it to your destination. Let's decide your destination before you get on the plane and hand select the perfect crew to get you there.

Wouldn't you agree that knowing the fees and risks associated with your investments would be critical information to know BEFORE you made any financial decision? That's what makes Accelerated Wealth Advisors different.

Chapter 3

Taking the Fear Out of Boarding the Plane

One of the biggest hurdles you may be facing is the feeling of not knowing what you don't know. It's a bit like trying to select an honest mechanic. You have an idea of what one should look like and you know where to find all kinds of mechanics but you usually go with the suggestion of a friend. Still, there is this nagging feeling that you may be getting taken to the cleaners.

Let's give you a little education so you can go into your interviews knowing what you're looking for.

First, you need to start with very different questions. The first question to any advisor should be, "Are you a fiduciary?" A fiduciary is legally bound to only make transparent decisions in the best interest of their client. The answer to this vital question should decide whether you continue the interview or declare it over. Some members of Congress and watchdog organizations have been attempting to bring this to the public discussion with great resistance from Wall Street community.

Simply stated, a fiduciary MUST and is LEGALLY REQUIRED to not only be transparent in ALL information and fees associated with his/her services, but is held ACCOUNTABLE for all recommendations made so that those recommendations are in the best interest of the client without regard to his fees or commissions.

Chances are, MOST of your experiences have been with broker/dealers. A broker/dealer is held only to a SUITABILITY requirement – meaning, their recommendations are suitable for the needs and desires their client has EXPRESSED.

There is a huge difference in the two.

At Accelerated Wealth Advisors, we are fiduciaries. We are RIA's – Registered Investment Advisors. Each of our RIA's holds a Series 65 license, which makes us Investment Advisor Representatives – IAR's. As fiduciaries, we are held to this higher standard.

Be aware! Some advisors are now wrapping themselves in a Certified Financial Planner (CFP) blanket and tout that they are fiduciaries. This is called a hybrid. Although they announce they are fiduciaries, they are not TRUE fiduciaries and are tethered to a broker/dealer whose interest they must first consider. They often have limited products that are put forth from the broker. See below for a chart of the difference.

BROKER (Registered Representative) Series 6, 63, and 7 Licenses	INDEPENDENT FIDUCIARY Series 65 or 66 Licenses
Paid commissions for selling funds	Paid flat fee for advice
Nondeductible commissions	Advisory fees (may be deductible)
Paid to sell	Legally bound to provide advice with disclosure of any conflicts
Suitability standard	**Fiduciary standard**
Offers broad array of products and services that must be approved by the employer and includes those with are proprietary	Ability to access all products and services
Constrained by employer	Usually independent
Acts as a custodian of investments	Usually uses third party custodian

Whose interest are they looking out for?

Let's take a new approach to building your financial plan. As wealth strategists, our job is to help you identify the areas where you are UNKNOWINGLY and UNNECESSARILY transferring your hard-earned wealth to others, and to plug those holes. There are three main areas that this occurs:

1. Taxes

2. Debt – Interest you pay on purchases

3. Losses and fees in the stock market

Asking what is your risk tolerance is another way of asking, "How much money can you afford to lose?" We take a different approach. We want to know your story, so we start by understanding:

- Who you are
- What your dreams are and what fuels your dreams
- What is keeping you awake at night
- What stage of life you are in?

We then utilize what we call Life Stage Planning and the Five Basket Strategy ™ to design a plan that is appropriate for your stage of life and is tailored to meet your *financial goals,* not your risk tolerance.

We focus on how to securely protect and grow your assets.

Our Process normally involves 4 meetings. Our goal is to hold these meetings in four consecutive weeks. *

- Discovery
- Diagnostics
- Design
- Delivery

We work on finding solutions, not on selling products. Our process is High Education – Low Tension. More than that, we have a comprehensive wealth building strategy.

Remember that plane that had a 57% chance of never arriving at its destination? When applied to the financial plan, that's usually because the different crew members aren't talking and communicating.

If you have started wealth planning, can you think of the last time your accountant spoke with your attorney? Have your estate planner and the person in charge of investments ever met? It's tough to build a comprehensive wealth strategy without large amounts of communication and one plan pointed at your goals.

Our approach is different

At Accelerated Wealth Advisors our goal is to build a comprehensive wealth strategy. The only way to do this is a collaborative approach involving a team of professionals with one shared goal; build the best possible wealth strategy plan for you.

The Accelerated Wealth Advisors Integrated Resource Network (IRN)

A teamwork approach is crucial to the creation of a successful comprehensive financial strategy. If you were undergoing surgery, you would not want the surgeon to be the only person in the room! Just like surgery, it takes a team of well-trained professionals working together to create a comprehensive financial strategy. Our Integrated Resource Network simplifies the process of navigating today's complex financial world by ensuring all aspects of your finances are connected.

Our clients typically have multiple professionals helping them with decisions that can impact their finances. The IRN facilitates communication and coordination of involved professionals ensuring that all aspects of your finances work together for your benefit.

Meet the members of your team. This is the crew that will get you to your dream destination. Imagine all of these professionals in one room with one item on their agenda, YOU and YOUR GOALS:

- Certified public accountant to provide tax planning and strategies to help you keep more of what you make
- Attorney to create estate plans
- Wealth strategist specializing in college planning and resources
- Wealth strategist to design safe asset strategies
- Lending specialist to provide real estate mortgage services and advice
- Banking specialist to assist with banking system and maximizing benefits in the system to your advantage
- Insurance professional to perform an insurance analysis for the purpose of protecting you, your family and the wealth you've built while it grows and develops.

Accelerated Wealth Advisors is not just another investment firm. We have a passion for people, businesses, and families. We want to see you achieve your financial goals and live the life you desire.

During the trying times of WWII Winston Churchill stated, "He who fails to plan, plans to fail."This is a quote often heard but rarely listened to. We are passionate about your plan! Here is how we plan to help you reach your goals.

Section II

4 D's to Accelerated Wealth

Chapter 4

The First D: The Discovery Phase

You may enter our offices with a ball sitting in the pit of your stomach because you are unsure of your financial picture. Some clients keep detailed notes and know where each and every dollar is. Most clients don't. This is what the first meeting is for. This meeting is called the Discovery Phase.

If what you thought you knew to be true turned out not to be so, when would you want to know? If there was a missing piece of information that was costing you money now or that would cause a significant problem or cost in your future, when would you want to find out about it? Today? 5 or 10 years from now? Never?

If that piece of information was a must-know fact, would you agree you would want to know about it before making any financial decision, especially one that put your money at risk?

That's what makes Accelerated Wealth Advisors different! We seek to identify all the critical facts necessary to make a sound financial decision that is in your best interest <u>before making that decision</u>.

Many times investors don't have a process to filter out myths and misconceptions to find out the must-know critical facts to make logical decisions for their future.

Do you know what questions to ask? Have you quantified hidden fees, taxes or risk issues? Have you made decisions based on myths, misconceptions, opinions or missing facts?

If you find out there are flaws or missing information in your decision making process you will quickly realize where money is falling through the cracks in your current planning, thus helping you make more informed financial decisions.

A visit to the physician tells us a lot about using a time-proven process to access our health and make decisions about what to do next. It is called the diagnostic approach. If our physician did not use this approach, we would most likely find a new doctor.

It goes something like this:

- We arrive at the doctor's office a few minutes early to fill out the requisite forms that ask for our insurance information and notations of any changes in our health. We are also asked for a full list of medications we are currently taking.
- After a brief (we hope) wait in the reception area, we are called and our vital signs are recorded: weight, blood pressure and temperature. We are then moved to an exam room where we have a brief wait (further hope) once again for the physician to arrive.
- The physician then greets us and begins to ask a series of questions about why we are here today and what is the nature of any problems we might be experiencing? She will review the history part of our charts. She then might ask us to sit on an exam table where she will perform a physical, all the while asking and probing about our complaints.
- After a careful exam and questions, she might order more tests like a blood draw, MRI, X-Ray or other tests to help her form a diagnosis.
- At last, either immediately or after receiving test results, she will complete a treatment plan based upon fact and logic. This plan will be offered in the best interest of the patient.

Well, what if it went a bit differently? What if when we arrived and were asked to fill out the questionnaire, we declined? What if we refused to have the vital signs done? What if when the doctor entered the room, we said, "Good day, doctor, thanks for taking the time to see me today. I won't need you to examine me. My problem is I've been experiencing some chest pain and a bit of lethargy.

I talked to my brother-in-law and spent some time with Dr. Google researching this thing. I know a guy at work who said he felt the same way but feels fine now. I really feel like this is my problem too. His doctor gave him a prescription for XYZ drug and man, he is feeling fine. So, could you just write me the same script and I'll be on my way? "

Of course no ethical physician would ever do such a thing and we would never tolerate a physician who did.

We are programmed to have a physician utilize the diagnostic approach to medicine to determine what might be wrong and to take action based on fact and logic, not on myths, misconceptions, misinformation or emotion. In short, we follow a process. A process finely tuned to separate myths and misconceptions and to give us information that will help us make a decision based upon fact and logic.

If we were not aware that taking a combination of medicines might be contraindicated and could result in a dangerous if not deadly result for us, when would you want to know? Today? Tomorrow? In a month? In five years? Never?

The physician uses a process to determine if this might be a deadly situation.

All of us that are successful in life have a process we have utilized in our businesses, our jobs and in raising our families. We are process-driven.

Pilots ALWAYS perform a walk-around of the plane checking the flaps, the rudder, the fuel and more BEFORE he gets in the plane to go on the flight.

The structural engineer ALWAYS follows a process to make sure that the materials utilized in the building of the bridge have the tolerances to withstand the winds or water currents and that the strength of the steel will withstand the loads of the projected weights.

Everyone that is successful has a process and they follow it daily, weekly, or minute-by-minute.

Yet in the world of financial planning, some people have come to accept that most of the time they don't even expect or understand what a process might look like to help us understand risk, fees, taxes or a host of other critical information to make a sound financial decision. Such a process should be based upon fact and logic — one that separates myth and misconception, and possible missing or wrong information or emotion — providing a set of questions to apply to any recommendations that will allow a decision based upon fact and logic. Without this process, we don't even know what questions to ask.

In short, Accelerated Wealth Advisors gives you a process. That's what makes us different. We are not the same old wine in a different bottle.

That's why we always begin with the Accelerated Wealth Review and the Discovery meeting.

Our Accelerated Wealth Review helps you discover if your current strategies match up with your future plans. <u>This proven process helps us create a sound plan based on facts and logic.</u>

We start the Discovery process by looking at the risk you might not be aware of in your portfolio and the fees that may or may not be transparent in your current situation.

Risk – Is the possible reward in line with the risk your current positions hold? Did your advisor quantify the risk? Is it correct for your stage of life? Is there a disconnect between what you thought you had and what the actual risk of those investments were?

Fees – A look at your financial statement will help us to determine what fees you are now paying. You may not have noticed some of these. We call them hidden fees and more often than not, especially in mutual funds and variable annuities, the hidden fees will be greater than the advisor fees. Have these ever been quantified for you?

Our Accelerated Wealth Review helps you implement the correct strategy to lower or eliminate your taxes and find money falling through the cracks now and in your future.

The second step is an income analysis to determine if you are using your income sources properly and in the most tax-efficient method. With the ever-increasing cost of inflation, we find out whether you have adequate income and liquidity to meet your future needs. Your actual inflation rate may be different from the government-quoted inflation rate as your rate is based on what you specifically spend money on.

The third step is a risk analysis to make sure that your investment risk exposure is one you are comfortable with and that it is in line with your life stage and with what we call Life Stage Planning.

Each investment product has a specific purpose where it may fit properly into someone's retirement planning. But without a complete review of your personal situation, risk tolerance, income needs, tax situation, long-term care needs, and estate and charitable desires, no one should offer an opinion on whether a specific product is right for you.

The discovery of your true needs and desires is the first step you should take, not the choice of investment products that historically many people have made as their first step.

Research shows people make poor decisions and thus receive low rates or incur losses because they have more risk than they are comfortable with. A simple set of questions will help us identify your true risk comfort level and possibly help you avoid losses you are not prepared to handle or were not aware of.

We want to know what keeps you up at night. Usually, it's the fear of the unknown. It is the "What if's?" It is the not knowing whether you have a properly structured financial plan.

In part, your fear is due to news reports predicting economic gloom and doom. It is also the vast amount of misinformation circulating regarding finances and economic impacts. Our first goal is to educate you, so that the monster in the closet seems a little less real. Our second goal is to actively involve you in the wealth strategy planning process, so that you understand your plan and have confidence in it.

Everyone has dreams and aspirations. For a wealth strategy plan to work, it has to take into account your individual dreams. The plan has to be able to provide the financial wherewithal to make these dreams reality and give you the money you want when you want it.

I know when I ask you what your financial goals are, I may get a blank stare. Often my client is thinking, "You're the financial advisor. Aren't you supposed to tell me?" Indeed, this is how many traditional financial planners work. The underlying concept doesn't work. A goal by definition must be personal to the individual setting the goal. Part of building a comprehensive wealth strategy is working with you to establish your goals. It's time for you to think about your life and your future.

I'm aware that most of your goals surround retirement. It's been my experience that when most clients think about their financial future, retirement is at the top of the list.

What kind of retirement do you want? Don't be satisfied with just not having to go to work every day. When you retire, you have to think of every day being a Saturday. At the very least, you may eat out more and want to really enjoy fine dining experiences. You'll want to go out more and travel. Maybe you'd like to tour the country or serve the local mission field. Whatever your retirement may look like to you, we can help you get there.

First, we can't build you a plan to get you where you're going until we know where you are. This can be a stressful situation for our clients because, maybe, you're not sure where everything is. It's ok. That's what we are here for!

We don't utilize a software package into which we plug in your numbers, and then it spits back a one-inch thick report based on hope. Instead we take a collaborative approach. With you we create a comprehensive plan based upon the stage of your financial life and the protection of the Five Basket Strategy, which we will cover soon. Each client's plan is unique to address his or her needs and desires.

Once we have gathered together and understand your current financial situation, it's time to move on to the second D, the Diagnostic Phase.

Bob and Angie: Accelerated Wealth Advisors in action: The first D: Discovery

Bob and Angie Barnes came to a seminar because they received a card in the mail. They knew one day they'd be one of the 10,000 people a day turning age 65 and they wanted to make sure they were in a good position to weather the storm. Bob and Angie had been hearing on the news about Social Security laws changing, and after seeing the questions in their head laid out on a card they wanted answers. Bob and Angie listened attentively during the workshop and stayed for a few minutes after to ask some questions. They learned bits of critical information they had never thought to ask about. The couple decided to visit the office to have their current portfolio checked. Was their current portfolio in a good position to finish the race protected and grow to retirement? They made the decision to visit with us the following week and came with their tax returns, current investment statements, and information on a trust they'd set up.

I greeted Bob and Angie Thursday afternoon in our reception area. They were both sipping on a coffee from our cappuccino bar and Bob had a freshly baked chocolate chip cookie half-eaten when I walked into the reception area. I glanced at the electronic welcome sign on the receptionist's desk and thought of the four couples we had already met with today. The Tibbets, a newly retired couple with plans to travel internationally and settle in Nebraska close to their new grandchildren; the Roush's, both a year from retirement and looking for a way to stretch their savings and relax from a long career as teachers; and the Johnson's, a young couple (32 and

28) wanting to know how to protect their future and build a stress-free retirement down the way. All so different, yet all with many of the same issues and concerns we see daily: Will I have enough savings to live comfortably in retirement? Will my spouse be protected if I should predecease her/him? What if I get ill? Who will take care of me? What will it cost? What if the market corrects again like it did in 2001 and 2007 - 2008? Will I be able to stay retired? What if inflation raises its ugly head? Will my Social Security and pension keep up? Will I have to work part time? The country is a mess. What if they raise taxes? When should I take Social Security and will it still be there when I need it?

In the many years I have been working in this industry, almost everyone has the same set of questions and concerns. The world is particularly unstable and the markets can be scary. What do we do to sleep at night? How do we make a plan that will indemnify the many risks we see on the horizon? What if, what if, what if?????

I approached the Barnes couple and reached out my hand to shake theirs. As we moved toward the conference room, I could see their nervousness and anticipation of what this meeting would hold. I'm sure they were thinking, "What will they try to sell me? How much will it cost? Is what they shared with us at the workshop too good to be true? We have a good advisor and we trust her, why should we change?"

In the conference room we began the Discovery process of our meetings. This is where we learn about the client, their hopes, dreams, concerns and issues. Like most couples we see, Bob and Angie had worked hard all their lives. He was a tenured professor at the University with over 30 years of service. She was an RN who worked in an extremely difficult and specialized area of the hospital, neo-natal intensive care. Both of them were ready to look at their retirement and what it might look like.

They knew they wanted to travel more, even internationally at times. Ireland, Scotland and Italy were the places in Europe they wanted to visit first. Angie had a dream to lie on the beach in Tahiti and to visit the gardens of Japan and eat lots of sushi. They wanted to spend some time with their son Keith in Seattle and go more often to St Louis to see Bridgett and the new grandbaby. Paul, their youngest child, would be in his last year of medical school and ready to begin an ENT residency. They knew he would be entering into an ever more intensive part of his education. They were proud of him and his accomplishments and wanted to take him on a vacation to Canada the spring before.

This is where I went to the board and drew the Financial Lifeline, or what we call Life Stage Planning. I had gone over this at the workshop and as I refreshed their memory, I asked them where they saw themselves on this timeline. Were they in Accumulation or Preservation with Growth or Distribution/Income? Both agreed they were in the Preservation with Growth Stage — or at least should be. Over the course of working with thousands of clients, we have found this timeline question, and the answer to it, to be the most important of all. When we showed Bob and Angie this simple graph, the light came on. What they want and what they actually have are two very different things.

Bob and Angie had other concerns as well. They never wanted to be in the position of being a burden to their children or grandchildren. They wanted to hope for the best, both of them in good health until the end, but they needed to plan for Long Term Care in case it was ever needed.

Bob's pension with the university was a good one – he would receive 60% of his current salary and he had contributed to a 403(b) for the last ten years that had grown to $425,000. Angie had no pension but had contributed to a 401(k) that was now worth $540,000. They also had saved over the years and had two stock accounts valued today at around $325,000. They had two small IRA Roth accounts, all in the market in mutual funds. Their savings and checking accounts totaled about $25,000.

We looked at options in Bob's pension. If he were to predecease Angie, she would receive 50% of his pension, or about $30,000 a year. Another way to look at it, her income would be reduced by $30,000 a year and she would also lose her life partner.

They told me the news in the economy seemed so hard to understand; one day the market was riding high and the next it would lose. Angie recounted their losses during the market corrections of 2001-2 and 2007-8. Their retirement accounts and savings in stocks had lost about 30% each time. They were pretty happy with that as some of their friends had lost as much as 50%.

We discussed the difference between "being ahead or down" in the market and taking the chips off the table and locking in the gains. If you've ever been to a casino, you know that you have never won until you go to the cashier and get the money the chips represent. You are only ahead or behind. Market accounts are just the same. When someone comes into my office and says they have "made 30% in the market this year or last," I ask them if they really made (or lost) money this last year, or are they just ahead or behind? It is an important distinction.

We went online to look at their Social Security benefits. The single greatest mistake we see in our practice is not understanding the complexity of Social Security and acting on emotion instead of looking at the possibilities clearly. Terms like, "Restricted Application" and "File and Suspend" are foreign to most of my clients. After running Bob and Angie's max report, we found that by just taking the Social Security benefits in the most advantageous manner, they would receive an additional $300,000 over their expected life span. Looking surprised, Bob turned to me and said simply, "Why have I never seen this before?"

We went through the rest of the meeting showing potential risks and hidden fees. Our visit had now run about an hour and a half and they were starting to get that *deer-in-the-headlights* look. I summed up what we had done in this first Discovery meeting and shared with them what we would do at the next visit, Diagnostics. We would take this discovered information and learn the following: about how to protect them from Losses and Fees in the Market; about Inflation; about Long Term Care; about Loss of Spouse or Pension Rescue; about the effect of

Taxes and Outliving their Savings; and about longevity. We would use a simple spreadsheet that we worked together to develop and make sure both spouses understood what options they had. Bob and Angie received the answers they were looking for and were amazed at the amount of education they'd received. Both were excited about the next meeting. They couldn't wait to learn more and be able to sleep at night once again.

SECTION III:
THE SECOND D: THE DIAGNOSTIC PHASE

Chapter 5

What You Have to Gain.

Now that we have a clear understanding of your financial picture we can begin to assess the strengths and weaknesses in your financial plan and recognize the opportunities available.

This step sets us apart from every other financial advisor firm. Have you met with a financial advisor and been asked the question, "So, tell me about your risk tolerance? Are you conservative, moderate, or aggressive when it comes to investing?" Have you been asked to fill out a questionnaire to help determine your "risk tolerance?" What you may not realize is you're really being asked, "How much can you stomach losing if we see another major market downturn--or even several of them--during your investment tenure or lifetime?"

The first question advisors should be asking, which clients should be asking themselves, isn't: "How much can you afford to lose?" It should be "What season of life am I in?" That is what Accelerated Wealth Advisors calls Life-Stage Financial Planning. To us, it's not about what you have to lose, it's about how we can help you prosper and grow right from where you are at any stage of life.

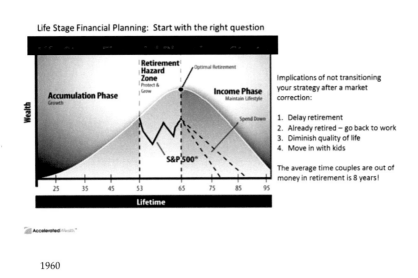

Life Stage Financial Planning: Start with the right question

1960

The Accumulation Phase

(From your first paycheck to 15 years before retirement)

The first phase requires a strategy that will put you in a place which maximizes everything you earn in your working years to prepare for retirement as well as for your legacy. The focus during this phase is growth. In this phase your work is providing your income and you begin to put away money for retirement. You have two things going for you. First is time horizon. Second is your human capital or earning potential. You have many years to work, earn, save, increase your income, and accumulate wealth.

The Retirement Hazard Zone ™

(about 14 years from retirement)

Also known as the RED ZONE!

This phase requires a much different strategy from the Accumulation Phase because your time horizon to retirement is much shorter. Priority one is protection. Growth, although still a consideration, is priority number two. Most people don't realize it, but this is where your retirement lifestyle is secured or lost. If the market has a strong correction, do you have the ability to recover your nest egg to the point that you're able to retire when you want to? Not if you hold on to the strategies used in the Accumulation phase. Again, this sets Accelerated Wealth Advisors apart. Very often, once a financial path is chosen and a plan put into place, it's left on "autopilot." We check and recheck your plan to make sure it is fitting your life and your life stage. For example, life insurance serves a different function when you're 30 with children as opposed to being 60 with grandchildren. It's important to transition your financial tools to match your life stages.

You must also protect your nest egg while still achieving growth for the future during this stage. We find the biggest mistakes folks make with their financial decisions is inaction. We call this "portfolio disconnect."

The Distribution Phase

(You're now retired)

The Distribution Phase has two parts. The first part of the distribution is when you are retired and instead of your work producing your income as in the accumulation phase, your assets along with pensions and social security are now producing your income. You begin to live off your life's work and your good financial planning decisions.

The number one fear in America today is running out of money before you run out of life. It's a subject we don't like to talk about or consider but an important one to examine. The risks of doing nothing or disconnecting from your portfolio risks include:

1. Work longer – pushing retirement back
2. Have to go back to work
3. Lower your retirement lifestyle
4. Risk running out of money
5. Move in with your kids
6. Leave nothing to your heirs

We make certain that our clients are informed and empowered, and have plans to ensure they don't have to worry during their retirement years. We will work alongside you to design a plan that shows you your retirement is going to last and turn into a legacy you can pass along to your heirs. We don't plan for you to die at a certain age. Our goal is to create a self-perpetuating comprehensive wealth strategy that will keep accumulating wealth throughout the years.

The planning that goes into a carefree distribution phase is extensive. You need to account for inflation, long-term care costs, medical care costs and other retirement killers.

The second part of the Distribution Phase is how your accumulated assets are distributed to loved ones, non-profits, and other areas of your choosing.

Once I have educated my clients on the three different phases of Life-Stage Financial Planning, they know which life-stage they are in and we can design a strategy that fits that life-stage.

As you can see, the Theory of Modern Portfolio Management is NOT an appropriate strategy for either of the last two phases of life. Let me say it another way. The old fashion pie chart made up of stocks, bonds, and mutual funds has failed repeatedly over the last decade. Monte Carlo style simulations show that a client using Modern Portfolio Management has a high degree of failure and risks running out of money. It doesn't matter how conservative you think your portfolio is; using an outdated model of financial planning is a recipe for disaster.
Financial planning should be dynamic and changing to fit your

current life stage, not a "set it and forget it" one-time plan. Accelerated Wealth Advisors offers the better way.

Once your current plan has been analyzed and your life stage assessed, we will begin to design your comprehensive wealth strategy. Part of that design is using the 5 Basket Strategy to be sure every aspect of your financial life is planned for and protected.

Chapter 6

Retirement Killers

Losses and Fees in the Market

As we discussed in the U.S. economic weather forecast, losses in the market from the tech bubble burst, 9/11, and the housing market collapse have decimated the portfolios of many retirees and want-to-be retirees. Even though most portfolios are back to, or just above, where they were in 2000, it has taken 14 years just to get back to even. The average Bear Market and a return to a Bull Market has historically been 17 years. The market has always come back and at Accelerated Wealth Advisors®, we firmly believe in the market as long as the Five Basket Strategy is in place.

There are some important pieces to understand; when someone is down in the market and loses 20-50% of the principal (their nest egg), the market has to come back not the 50% it lost, but about 90% just to get that person back to EVEN. If you have retired, you are no longer putting in part of your paycheck, and it will seem like forever until you are back to where you were when the market corrected. Many people have been forced to continue to work in an attempt to make up the shortfall which, by the way, is probably not possible. Instead of relaxing on the beach, many seniors now have part-time jobs. In addition, the hidden fees and costs of investing have taken an additional bite out of an already wounded portfolio.

Poor Social Security Planning

Social Security is as important to understand as your IRA. When and how you take Social Security may be the single most important decision you make in your retirement. The Social Security system is complex and unless you have a good guide, you are likely not to be aware of the many ways to capitalize on this pension. The people who help you at the Social Security office are not ALLOWED to advise you on the best strategy. And indeed it is a strategy that can result in your receiving as much as $200-400,000 more during your retirement lifetime if you just know when to take it and how to take it.

Accelerated Wealth Advisors will create a Social Security Maximization Report and work together with your wealth strategy to find the best way to receive the most from this pension fund that you contributed so much to over your lifetime. Don't leave this to chance or decide on an emotional response.

Loss of Spouse

Losing a husband or wife is a devastating experience that many of us will have to face. According to the latest U.S. Census figures, about 40 percent of women and 13 percent of men who are 65 and older are widowed. The loss of a spouse, for most people, is one of the most painful life events. It can also be one of the most economically threatening events if the spouse who dies was the primary breadwinner during life. Social Security will graciously give the surviving spouse an increase in monthly benefits. This increase may be as much as 100% of the deceased spouse's benefit. The catch is, the survivor only gets that one check. The check the surviving spouse was previously receiving stops. In some families that can mean a loss of 1/3 or more of household income. Also, depending on the elections made when everyone was well, pension or annuity income may be lost or reduced. Not only do you have the emotional issues associated with losing a spouse that you have raised children with and done everything with for thirty years or more, but now you have to deal with what could be a greatly reduced income.

Taxes

Of course, there is one thing as certain as death – taxes. Most people don't realize that we are in a historically LOW tax period. Since the inception of the IRS in 1913, the average tax on the highest adjusted gross income AGI, has been 58%! At the present with the rate just over 39%, we are getting a bargain! With the looming American debt crisis, Congress is looking for new and creative ways to tax. Historically, seniors have been the recipient of tax breaks. This is primarily because they make up the largest U.S. voting sector, and they do actually show up and vote. They may have preferential treatment in some cases, but they certainly don't have tax amnesty. As Congress gets more pressed to raise revenue, one thing is certain – taxes aren't going down, no matter who is President or in Congress. The largest impact on future tax rates are the baby boomers themselves. Medical advances help us to live longer, although with more and more expensive care. Programs such as Medicare, Medicaid and the Prescription Drug Plan are stretched to their limits. With no plan for future funding of these programs, many believe Congress will have no choice but to raise taxes or find deductions to reduce. What are called Unfunded Liabilities are the greatest danger to your retirement plan. As is the case in most of the Retirement Killers, no one can predict if and when they may occur, but by utilizing the wealth strategies employed by Accelerated Wealth Advisors® our clients are prepared with a plan. People don't plan to fail; they fail to plan.

Inflation

At 5% inflation, if you are currently living on $50,000 per year, in 10 years you will need $81,445; in 20 years you will need $132,665; and in 35 years $275,801. That's what inflation does. Based on longevity, if you live 25, 30, 35 years in retirement and we see inflation do what it's done here, will your portfolio keep up with inflation? Will your withdrawals keep up with inflation?

If you need this much at retirement		...you'll need this much		
Annual Inflation	*Current Income*	*In 10 years*	*In 20 Years*	*In 35 Years*
3%	$50,000	$67,196	$90,306	$140,693
5%	$50,000	$81,445	$132,665	$275,801
7%	$50,000	$98,358	$193,484	$533,829

Average historical return rates: 1990's – 3%, 1980's – 5%, 1970's – 7%. The average inflation rate from 1926-2007 was 3.1%. Source: Morningstar.com

Longevity

The good news – we're living longer. Here's the bad news – we're living longer. This creates a challenge to a retiree's portfolio. The graph below shows the chances of outliving your retirement income and the probability of survival beyond age 65. If you are a retired couple, both age 65, the likelihood one of you will live 30 years in retirement is 36%. So roughly, there is more than a 1 in 3 chance that one of you will live 30 years in retirement. So if you only plan for say 10, 15, or even 20 years, there's a good chance you could come up short.

Life expectancy from age 65

You may live longer than you expect			
People are living longer because they're healthy, active, and taking better care of themselves.			
	65-year-old man	65-year-old woman	65-year-old couple
50% chance of living to age:	85 years	88 years	92 years
25% chance of living to age:	92 years	94 years	97 years

To show how important this is, if you withdraw just 1% more than your planned withdrawal rate, you can go broke before you die. It is a mathematical truth. This is why accuracy is so critical – because the razor thin margin between 1% too much and getting it right could literally mean the difference between poverty and financial security, the difference between living independently and having to move in with the kids.

When I sit down with people, I ask them, "What withdrawal rate do you feel is sustainable?" I usually get a variety of answers. On average I hear the rates of 4%, 5% or 6%. And, they may be right, if they say "5%" and only live to age 75.

However, even looking at a portfolio that is 50% stocks, 40% bonds, and 10% treasury bills like the one shown here, notice the impact of just increasing the withdrawal rate by 1% up to 6% - and another 1% up to 7% - and another... Can you imagine what would happen if this portfolio was entirely in cash or fixed income? This shows that if someone is too conservative, their likelihood of running out of money is significantly greater because their portfolio can't keep up with their withdrawal rates. This is especially true when you add in the impact of inflation and longevity. And what if the market corrects severely as it has done twice in the last fourteen years? Would a 40-50% market loss change your lifestyle in retirement? Would you be OK living on half of what you had planned?

This is one of the key things we help our clients figure out, and it's why we recommend working with a qualified professional – an independent fiduciary. For this reason, it is especially important to use investment strategies that balance a sustainable withdrawal rate with the right measure of risk, and that take inflation into consideration. Balancing these factors is critical to help ensure you don't run out of money before you run out of life.

Long-Term Care – You either allocate some of your assets or you allocate ALL of your assets

A myth we often see with those who have done very well is, "I will self-insure for long term care. I don't want a long term care policy, they're expensive!" This may be misinformation or incorrect.   Often, by just moving an asset that is not being utilized for income to a different 'pocket,' one can have the protection for long-term care, if needed, yet keep the assets liquid and growing.

Wouldn't you agree that if there were a way to make sure you and your spouse had long-term care (if you ever needed it) and at the same time avoided the costly yearly premiums that make up most long-term care policies, that would be critical, must-know information? See Chapter 9

Chapter 7

Reducing Tax Liability

In an earlier chapter, we briefly touched on Stealth and Phantom Income taxes. During the review process, taxes and how to possibly decrease the impact of this phantom income are the first part of the Discovery process. While Phantom Income Tax does not affect everyone, it will at some point affect you if you have non-qualified funds invested in mutual funds and may be puzzling. The basic definition of phantom revenue is any income that is reported to the Internal Revenue Service for tax purposes but is not actually received by the entity or individual purportedly receiving it.

If the loss on paper is larger than the income distribution you received, this is Phantom Income taxation. On paper, you lost money for the year, yet you paid taxes on it.

Phantom Income Taxes in retirement occurs when you own investments like stocks, bonds or mutual funds in non-qualified accounts. If they produce interest, dividends or gains, you pay taxes – on earnings you never even used.

Even if you don't use the money to live on, and are reinvesting it for retirement or legacy, you still get taxed now.

And more importantly, even if your account lost value on paper you wind up paying this income tax this year. It can also cause double taxation on your Social Security.

Let's say a few years back you sat down with your financial advisor or broker and you invested $500,000. Five years later that account now has a value of $425,000. You take the statement to your advisor and you ask, "I'm a little confused. We gave you a chunk of our nest egg several years ago, we haven't taken any distributions and it's now worth $425,000."

And the broker says, "It's okay. Don't worry, Bob, because this is just a loss *on paper*."

Then January comes rolling along, you open up your mailbox and there's a 1099 tax form for a distribution of $15,000. And you take this 1099 tax form to your accountant and you say,

"What is this $15,000 distribution?"

Your tax advisor explains to you that during the year, the mutual fund manager sold off stocks at a gain and by federal law that gain has to be passed onto you in the form of a distribution.

And you say, "But I never even got a check in the mail. There was no distribution to me."

And the accountant says, "I understand that. But it's the way the tax system is structured. However, there's a little bit of good news: the income tax rate on that distribution is at an all-time low 15%."

Picture this. You're sitting in front of your accountant. You now have to cut a check to Uncle Sam for $2,250 on an account that lost value that cranked out a distribution you never even saw.

And in the years that Wall Street goes downwards or sideways, sometimes many years in a row (2015 being a great example), this tax could be $10,000 or more. All on what we call phantom income. That's money you pay taxes on but from which you never received a true distribution.

Wouldn't you agree that Phantom Income and how it affects your taxation is one of those critical must-know facts that you should be aware of if you are to make SOUND financial decisions?

To address the potential impact of taxation, we employ a multitude of strategies. One we commonly use has to do with asset location. Asset location is a tax minimization strategy that takes advantage of the fact that different types of investments get different tax treatments. Using this strategy, we help our clients determine which securities should be held in tax-deferred accounts and which securities should be held in taxable accounts in order to help maximize after-tax returns.

The best location for an investor's assets depends on a number of different factors including financial profile, prevailing tax laws, investment holding periods, and the tax-and-return characteristics of the underlying securities. Tax-efficient strategies need to be taken into consideration when developing effective wealth management strategies.

Tax Time Bombs

Most American investors have at least one, if not more, tax time bombs in their portfolios. Most people don't even hear the sound of the ticking. Why? Many of these time bombs have been disguised for years as best planning practices for saving taxes. The time bombs are your tax deferred assets. The most common tax deferred assets are:

- 401(K), 403(b), 757 accounts
- IRA

- SEP & Simple

As Americans, we are taught from elementary school that taxes are bad. This is the reason why we are not still English citizens. From our very first paystub we were introduced to our business partner – the United States of America. The more we made, the more Uncle Sam made. As we made more, we wanted to give Uncle Sam less. Congress was more than happy to give us this option. After all, it would cause more Americans to get excited about saving money. The worker could put aside money and defer the payment of income tax. The key word many people overlook in that last sentence is the word <u>defer</u>. "Defer" by definition means to postpone, not to avoid.

We will give the Congresses of the 70's who first enacted tax deferral laws the benefit of the doubt for the purpose of this discussion. The policy behind tax deferral was to allow the working taxpayer to create a savings fund with pre-tax money. The taxpayer would then have a resource to draw upon after retirement when they would be in a lower tax bracket. The fallacy here is, most people never arrive at that lower tax bracket. In part, this has to do with people working longer and having other investment income. Also, Congress has restructured the rates several times since the 1970's.

When Congress discovered that individuals were leaving money in tax-deferred accounts, they came up with the idea of the required minimum distribution (RMD.) This law forces seniors at age 70 ½ to take out a minimum amount based upon their life expectancy. If a person lived until their exact life expectancy, they would have withdrawn 100% of the account.

Many tax advisors counsel clients to take only the RMD from their tax-deferred assets unless they have an absolute need for the money. This strategy still involves postponement – not just of the tax itself, but of the calculation of the tax.

During the Discovery portion of our visits, we often ask our clients, "Who is your partner in your IRA or 401(k)?" They will usually answer, "I don't have a partner," or "my spouse." We ALL have a partner and he is greedy. Think of it this way. A farmer goes to the seed mill to get his corn seed to plant the crop for the year. When he is presented with the $1,000.00 bill, he is told by the clerk that there will be no tax on the seed under a new law. The tax on seed had previously been an outrageous 10%. This excites the farmer. He just saved $100! He plants the seed, fertilizes, weeds and waits. Finally, it is time to harvest the crop. It was a great growing year, and it is a bumper crop. He smiles the whole way to the mill. When the clerk hands him his check for the crop, the farmer notices a huge problem. Given the yield the farmer expected about $10,000. The check is for $9,000. When he questions the clerk, the clerk says, "Yep. They moved the 10% tax from the seed to the crop." Your partner is Uncle Sam, and he will make sure he gets his share.

This problem, like most, will not get better with time. Under the U.S. Constitution, Congress is given the power to tax. Congress has proven they fully understand how to use this power. Over the last century, the personal income tax rate has been as high as 93% on the highest adjusted gross incomes and has averaged 58%. There are many justifications for increasing taxes, including Social Security, Medicare, and Medicaid—all which directly benefit seniors. The reality is our country has a debt crisis that continues to get worse. There are two ways to close that gap: eliminate spending or increase taxes and reduce deductions. Given the situation, including today's relatively low tax rates, tax increases are inevitable.

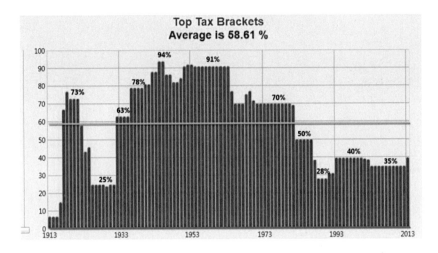

It may be time to rethink the RMD. Later we will talk about how you can defuse your tax time bombs by repositioning them into assets that will provide you income and security in your retirement. If you don't defuse the tax time bombs before your death, they will become part of your estate plan where they will continue to tick. We will also talk about ways to defuse the bomb in your estate plan.

The Certified Public Accountant's role as part of the Integrated Resource Network is to make sure that all legal tax breaks are fully utilized. This is crucial to stop wealth drain. Tax time bombs are only one of the potential sources of tax-related wealth drain. Several independent studies over the years have confirmed that the majority of Americans don't cheat on their taxes other than to cheat themselves. They fail to take completely acceptable deductions that are allowed under the law. It is the role of the CPA on the Integrated Resources Network to identify these drains and help plug them. Every dollar that doesn't have to be paid out in taxes is one less that you have to earn or pull from your investments.

In the next chapter we will discuss how and when you take Social Security, and how the position of your other assets can make a difference in your retirement.

Chapter 8

Strategies to Maximize your Lifetime Social Security Benefit

Social Security income is a critical source of income to most retired individuals. Some have recently tried to paint Social Security as an Entitlement rather than a BENEFIT that you earned, just like your pension. You paid into this program and you SHOULD benefit and not be made to feel like it is an entitlement.

Despite the doom and gloom reports of many media outlets, the Social Security System, while certainly not healthy, is not going to be revoked by the government. Yes, there is likely to be further restructuring, but the system as it applies to retired individuals and those within 10 years of their retirement date is highly unlikely to change. These individuals make one of the biggest blocks of active voters. Approving changes which threaten this group's fixed income would mean the end of the political career for any elected official who was involved or voted yes.

According to information compiled by the Social Security Administration, Social Security is one of your largest retirement assets making up on average 64.8% of the total retired household income. In addition to being mandatory, it's the best annuity money can buy. Every dollar you increase your Social Security income means less money you'll have to spend from your nest egg to supplement your income. The key is to maximize your Social Security benefits. While everyone's situation is truly different, there are three key maximization factors:

> Your age when you begin to draw benefits
> Your marital status
> Your lifestyle

Social Security as an Asset Class

Social Security benefits are as important as — and should be viewed the same as — any other asset class such as 401(k)'s,

IRA's, Annuity's, etc. If one begins to understand the power of an increasing income, and a lifetime income at that, the distinction of Social Security being another of your important retirement assets will begin to make sense. In the chart below, see how the average income from SS can be the same as having an asset valued at close to a million dollars.

In 2014 the Average Monthly Social Security Benefit was $1,900

➢ $1,900 X 12 Months = $22,800 per Year

To put this in perspective:

❑ The average Lifetime Annuity Payment beginning at 66 is 5%.

➢ **$456,000 at 5% = $22,800** of Guaranteed Lifetime Income

❑ When taking into consideration the past two market corrections of 2000-2002 and 2007-2009, the 4% Rule would have experienced a 94% failure rate. In a recent report Morning Star advises retirees to use 2.65% of their investments each year to calculate their retirement income.

➢ **$860,377 at 2.65% = $22,800**

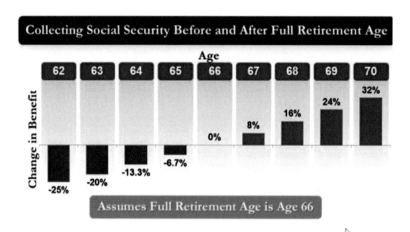

Collecting Social Security Before and After Full Retirement Age

Assumes Full Retirement Age is Age 66

At What Age Should You Begin to Draw Benefits?

This is the most important decision you can make in maximizing your Social Security benefits. Simply put, the longer you delay drawing benefits, the larger the amount you are entitled to receive. The earliest you can begin to draw benefits before your full retirement age (FRA) is at age 62. If you do this, you will be significantly and permanently reducing the amount that you are eligible to receive. There are instances where income constraints make this unavoidable, but it is in general a very bad idea. If you can wait to draw benefits until after your FRA when you are 70, you could increase your benefit by as much as 43%.

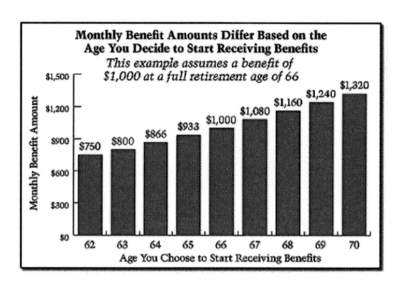

Monthly Benefit Amounts Differ Based on the Age You Decide to Start Receiving Benefits

This example assumes a benefit of $1,000 at a full retirement age of 66

Adjusting the full retirement age is one way Congress has tried to fix Social Security. In fairness, Congress has tried to implement this change gradually over time so as to not impact individuals who are nearing retirement age or who are already retired. See the chart below for the current FRA's. The maximum benefit rate for 2015 is $2,663.00.

Year of birth	Full retirement age	Percentage of full benefits received at 62	Yearly increase if retirement delayed beyond FRA
1937 or earlier	65	80%	-
1938	65 and 2 months	79.1	-
1939	65 and 4 months	78.3	-
1940	65 and 6 months	77.5	-
1941	65 and 8 months	76.6	7.5%
1942	65 and 10 months	75.8	7.5
1943 – 1954	66	75	8
1955	66 and 2 months	74.1	8
1956	66 and 4 months	73.3	8
1957	66 and 6 months	72.5	8
1958	66 and 8 months	71.6	8
1959	66 and 10 months	70.8	8
1960 or later	67	70	8

If you do elect to delay drawing benefits beyond 65, you are still entitled to receive Medicare. You should start that enrollment process three months before your 65th birthday.

If one of the things keeping you up at night is not knowing for certain what your Social Security benefits will be, there is a way to put that fear to rest. The Social Security Administration website contains a tool called the "Retirement Estimator." After you enter your basic information, it will generate a report showing your monthly benefits at each age after 62.

It may seem simple to understand: The longer you wait to take your Social Security benefits at your full retirement age, the more money you'll get every month. But in our practice, time and time again, we see people that take their Social Security

Benefits based upon an emotional decision (I earned it, and I want it now!) or on misinformation or misconceptions on how this important retirement income can benefit you the most.

Those benefits make up 40 percent of all post-retirement personal income, according to the Nationwide Retirement Institute. Yet only 15 percent of us elect to wait to full retirement age to take benefits, and just 10 percent start taking Social Security after 70.

All told, more than half of Americans start collecting Social Security at 62 – and four out of five women.

The "wait to take" is especially important, given increasingly extended lifespans. Women who reach 65 are expected to live to 86, according to government tables, and 25 percent will live past 90. Men who reach 65 can expect to live to 83.

How Does Marriage Affect Social Security?
Before you can make an informed decision regarding when to begin drawing benefits, it is essential that you understand how marriage impacts Social Security. As a spouse you can claim the higher of the benefits based upon your work record, or a spousal benefit of 50% of your spouse's Social Security benefit. There are three critical factors that affect Social Security benefits for spouses:

1. Length of Marriage
2. Work History

3. The Age of Both Spouses

Spousal and survivor benefits cause some of the greatest confusion when it comes to Social Security benefits. Often representatives at Social Security are hard pressed to accurately explain how all of these factors interplay. The standard answer is, "Our computers are programed to ensure you get the maximum benefit to which you are entitled." While this is fine answer, it is far from an explanation.

To understand the answer, you first have to understand how benefits are calculated. You need 10 years of work history (40 credits – one per quarter) to qualify for your Social Security benefits. The benefit will be based on an average of the 35 years in which you earned the most. Higher lifetime earnings equal higher benefits. If there are years in which you earned low or no income, your benefit amount may be lower than if you had worked steadily. Historically, women have taken substantially more time out of the workforce to care for families than men. Depending on the length of the work hiatus, this can substantially impact the wife's benefits. Among the women retirees of today, there is a large subset of women who never worked outside the home and are entitled to no benefit of their own.

Many women actually qualify for a higher benefit based upon their husband's work history. Indeed, when applying for benefits the computer will determine automatically which way your benefits will be greater. However, to receive benefits based upon a spouse's work history:
    The basics:

➢ Both spouses must be at least age 62.

➢ They need to have been married for at least one year or have a dependent child together.

➢ The spouse with the longer work history or higher estimated benefit must actually apply for Social Security retirement benefits in order for the other spouse to collect. However, he/she can then choose to delay collecting benefits until later, when he or she may qualify for a higher benefit.

The divorced and never remarried can claim against his or her ex-spouse's record:

➢ You are divorced from your spouse and unmarried, and you were married for at least 10 years. Your ex-husband must be eligible for benefits. If he is eligible but is not currently receiving benefits, you can still qualify for spousal benefits if you have been divorced for two or more years. Tip: you will need your former spouse's Social Security Number.

➢ However, if your ex-husband is deceased and you are currently unmarried, you may collect benefits as early as age 60 as a surviving divorced spouse. If he is deceased and you are disabled, you can collect benefits as early as age 50.

The divorced and remarried can claim against his or her ex-spouse's record:

➤ If you divorce and remarry you will be entitled to benefits on your first spouse's work record only if your second husband is deceased. The second marriage must also have been at least 10 years. Accelerated Wealth Advisors will determine which of your former spouse's work histories results in the higher award.

Death
➤ If your husband passes away, you can collect survivor's benefits as early as age 60. You are eligible to receive his full Social Security benefit amount.

> ➤ If your ex-husband is deceased and you remarry before age 60 (or 50 if you are disabled), you cannot receive survivor's benefits unless the latter marriage ends (whether it be through death, divorce, or annulment). If you remarry after age 60, you can continue to receive benefits on your former husband's Social Security record. However, if your current husband is also a Social Security beneficiary and you would receive a larger benefit from his work record than you would from your former husband's record, you should apply for spousal benefits on your current husband's record. You cannot receive both benefits.

> ➤ Regardless of your age or marital status, if you are caring for your deceased ex-spouse's child or children, you would be eligible to receive benefits for raising

them until they are 16 years old. These children can then continue to receive benefits based on the deceased parent's work record until they are 18 or 19, as long as they are unmarried. If a child is still a full-time student (no higher grade than grade 12) when they turn 18, they can continue to receive benefits until 2 months after they turn 19 or until they graduate, whichever comes first. Children who are disabled can also continue to receive benefits after they turn 18 years old.

If your spouse applies before his or her FRA, it can have a significant impact on your spousal benefit. The Social Security Agencies Retirement Estimator also performs this calculation based upon your individual information.

- At age 65, you would receive 45.8% of your spouse`s benefit.
- At age 64, you would receive 41.7% of your spouse`s benefit.
- At age 63, you would receive 37.5% of your spouse`s benefit.
- At age 62, you would receive 35% of your spouse`s benefit.

If your spouse had the higher benefit amount, at the time of his or her death your benefits will automatically be recalculated as follows:

- Widow or widower, full retirement age or older – 100 percent of the deceased worker's benefit amount;

- Widow or widower, age 60 until full retirement age – 71½ to 99 percent of the deceased worker's basic amount;
- Disabled widow or widower aged 50 through 59 – 71½ percent;
- Widow or widower, any age, caring for a child under age 16 – 75 percent.

How Does Lifestyle Effect Social Security?

Lifestyle affects Social Security decisions in many ways. The first and most obvious way is spending habits. If Social Security is going to be your primary source of retirement income, is it enough to keep you in the lifestyle to which you have grown accustomed? If not, do you have other retirement income streams that will make up the cash shortfall? If not, are you willing to adjust your lifestyle to your new circumstances? If not, how are you making up the cash shortfall?

There are two less obvious ways that your lifestyle and life circumstances impact your decision regarding when to begin drawing Social Security. The first question is, when do you intend to retire? If you continue to work, in most cases you should delay drawing benefits.

If you elect to start drawing benefits before reaching your full retirement age, they will be reduced by $1 for every $2 of annual earnings above $15,720. If you reach full retirement age in 2015, the earnings limit is $41,880 through the month before your birthday. Above that, the reduction is $1 for every $3. If you continue to work, there are no earnings limits after reaching full retirement age and you will receive your full benefit.

Age	Benefit Reduction	2015 Earned Income Limits
Age 62 Until Full Retirement Age	Lose $1 of benefit for every $2 earned above limit	$15,720
Year of Full Retirement Age	Lose $1 for every $3 earned above limit	$41,880
After Full Retirement Age	No benefit reduction	No limit

The second question is how will your benefits be taxed when combined with your other retirement income? Social Security is potentially taxable depending on your total annual income. Annual income includes job earnings, pensions, investment interest, even tax-exempt interest, as well as other sources such as annuity payments.

There are different thresholds depending on your filing status and provisional income. See the chart below for more information. If your preliminary adjusted gross income falls within these thresholds, a portion of your Social Security benefit must be included as taxable income on your federal tax return.

	No Taxes on SS Benefits	Up to 50% of SS Benefits Are Taxed	Up to 85% of SS Benefits Are Taxed
Single	Income <$25,000	$25,000–$34,000	Income >$34,000
Married, Filing Jointly	Income <$32,000	$32,000–$44,000	Income >$44,000

Provisional Income is an important part of how the taxes on your Social Security are calculated. See the chart below. Accelerated Wealth Advisors will help you to determine how to structure your income to have the impact of social security taxes minimized.

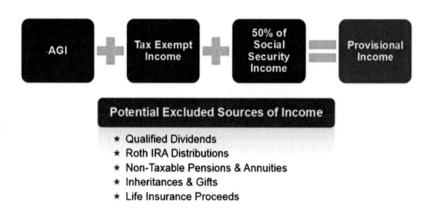

Potential Excluded Sources of Income

★ Qualified Dividends
★ Roth IRA Distributions
★ Non-Taxable Pensions & Annuities
★ Inheritances & Gifts
★ Life Insurance Proceeds

A Word of Caution
The Retirement Estimator tool on the Social Security Agency's website is both user friendly and accurate; however, it cannot take the place of professional financial advice. You need to review this information with your financial professional and consider it in light of the rest of your financial picture. Theoretically, a couple in Ohio and a couple in Wyoming may have identical situations that lead to the same exact reports from the Retirement Estimator. That does not mean that they should make the exact same choice as to when to begin to draw Social Security.

Medicare/Medigap

An important part of your retirement plan is how Medicare and a Medigap policy will affect your needed income. Many Accelerated Wealth Advisors clients believe that the cost of Medicare and the portion that Medicare part B doesn't cover will be low cost. This is not true. Medicare part B (available at the age of 65, it covers doctor visits, etc.) has a true cost to it. Depending upon your income, the monthly cost can be as much as $335 per month. Couple that with a Medigap policy (which covers the portion Medicare doesn't) that has an average cost of $300 per month. The combined cost for these can be between $8,000-$11,000 per person or individual. A couple should plan about $22,000 per year for healthcare. Accelerated Wealth Advisors will help you to navigate the Medicare puzzle and make sure you make the best choices.

Chapter 9

Planning for Long Term Care Costs

If you're not allocating a portion of your retirement investments for long term care, then you're allocating all of it. I know a lot of people don't like to talk about this, but another factor that has to be considered when it comes to having a longer life expectancy is that medical care is expensive.

According to a Genworth study, in Colorado where our corporate office is located, the average costs in 2015 for assisted living was more than $45,000 a year growing at 2% a year. The annual cost of a private room in a nursing home was nearly $93,531 growing at 3% year, and home health aides averaged $19 per hour. These are just averages. Plus, we're not even considering the cost of other things like medication and doctor visits. We all know medical costs don't seem to be going anywhere but up. After 100 days, Medicare no longer will cover the costs of skilled nursing. Then you are on your own.

The Continuum of Care

The U.S. Census Bureau estimates that 14.1% of the population is currently over 65. For seniors and their families, understanding the continuum of care is vital when making long-term care choices. The goal of this article is to provide a brief overview of the options:

At-Home Independent Living: A senior at this stage is capable of living in his or her own home without the need of personal care or nursing assistance. Typically, this person is capable of driving, preparing meals, handling their finances, and other day-to-day errands and chores.

Independent Living in a Continuing Care Retirement Community (CCRC): The last 20 years have seen a surge in the building of independent housing in continuing care retirement communities. These units are often built as duplexes or cluster homes (with up to five individual units sharing a common roof.) Some communities also offer single-family homes; others offer apartments. The resident pays an entry fee and a monthly maintenance fee. If a resident moves or dies prematurely, usually part of the fee is refundable. The resident lives independently in his or her unit, however the CCRC is responsible for outdoor maintenance. Basic interior maintenance is usually included in the monthly maintenance fee. As communities compete for new residents, the services provided have improved and increased. Some communities provide services ranging from recreational facilities to technical support.

At Home Living with Assistance: In this situation, the individual is still capable of living in his or her own home or an independent living unit within a CCRC, but needs assistance with some or many activities of daily living. This individual may need assistance with transportation, grocery shopping, cleaning, maintenance, or cooking. He or she may also need assistance with personal hygiene, medication management, and finances. At first, this assistance usually comes from family or friends. As the need for support increases, often families elect to bring in paid providers. This help can be in the form of a private individual or personal care company. A word of caution: if you are employing the individual directly, there are tax and possible insurance requirements. If you use an agency, you pay more, but the agency takes care of these requirements.

Personal Care Homes: Personal care homes are designed for seniors who still function well, but need assistance with personal care. Many seniors and families find this to be a better option than having the services provided in the senior's home. It is often more cost effective. Personal care homes offer 24/7 supervision, which can be vital if an individual has a history of falling or is in the early stages of a dementia type illness. Seniors living in these settings often continue to drive and provide for many of their own needs.

A word of caution, many states do not regulate personal care homes. This is not necessarily bad, as it keeps the cost down, but you should know whether your state has oversight authority. If your state does not regulate personal care homes, you should be very careful when selecting a home to make sure proper health and safety protocol is followed. Also, in non-regulated states, there is no requirement that the operator of a personal care home has any medical background or medical staffing on the premises.

Assisted Living Facilities: Unlike personal care homes, assisted living facilities are almost always regulated by the state. In some facilities, the resident has a bedroom and bathroom. In other facilities, the resident lives in an apartment type setting complete with a kitchen, living room, bedroom, and sometimes a guest room or den. Units can be single resident, or shared with a roommate in order to defray the cost. In this environment, the resident often needs assistance with many of the activities of daily living including personal hygiene and medication management, but they do not need regular skilled nursing care. Assisted living is typically half the cost of skilled nursing care, so the goal is to maintain the resident in this setting as long as possible.

Skilled Nursing Care: When an individual can no longer be cared for in his or her home or at an assisted living facility, the next step is a skilled nursing facility. This is what most people think of as a traditional nursing home. In 2012, the national average cost of caring for an individual in a nursing home was $81,000 a year, making it the most expensive option in the continuum of care. After a hospitalization due to an illness or broken bone, a senior may go to a facility briefly for a rehabilitation period. Medicare usually pays for rehab stays. Permanent residents must either pay privately for nursing homes or spend down their assets until they are Medicaid qualified.

Last year the Medicaid program paid approximately $143 billion dollars for skilled nursing care. This is the driving force behind the governmental mandates to give seniors both more options and more affordable options.

Paying for Long-Term Care

When planning for long-term care, a commonly asked question is, "Do I need long term care insurance?" The honest answer to this question for most people is: No. Long-term care insurance is insurance that will help pay for your care at home or in an institutional setting.

Long-term care policies have been around in one form or another since the 1970's. In theory, it sounds like a great idea; however, over time it has become apparent that long term care insurance premiums are probably not the best use of your money. This is true for several reasons. First, under the majority of the policies, the premium is not refundable. In other words, if you die without needing care, your estate doesn't get any money back. Second, over time premiums increase. When seniors purchase these policies, they are told their individual premiums can never be increased. This is true, but the premiums for your group can be increased and often are. As premiums increase, many seniors elect to drop the policy because it is no longer affordable. They do not receive any of their premiums back. Third, as claims have started to come in against the policies sold in the 70's and 80's many of the big insurance companies have elected to stop writing long-term care insurance. Some companies have elected to "buy out" the contracts by essentially returning premiums to the insured. Others have defaulted on their coverage obligations.

There are far better ways to provide for your long-term care other than traditional long-term care insurance.

Because long-term care insurance is expensive — and because in many cases you will not qualify for it — at Accelerated Wealth Advisors®, we utilize a system of locating a portion of your assets into the Long-Term Care basket. If you have a care issue, those funds are now leveraged to provide 2-3 times the original amount located. They can be tax- deductible now. We call it Live, Quit or Die. You're covered in all circumstances.

If you LIVE a great long life and at some point need some form of long-term care assistance, it is available to you leveraged and tax-free. If you Quit and want to use the funds for something else, they are all available. If you DIE the growing fund passes to your beneficiaries tax-free.

At Accelerated Wealth Advisors we utilize our Five Basket Strategy (see chapter 11). You should create one basket for long-term care. This basket will hold a reserve to fund long-term care. If it is never used, it becomes part of your legacy. Also, money can be drawn from your private pension fund and the infinite bank (see chapter 13) to fund the care. Your infinite bank holds a life insurance policy. The ideal policy for the infinite bank is one that allows you to draw out excess funds tax-free for end-of-life care and long- term care.

If you are an eligible military veteran, you and your spouse can receive up to $33,000 of TAX-FREE income per year. For a surviving spouse, the amount is over $12,000 toward your long-term care expense.

Chapter 10

The Death of a Spouse

Probably the most significant emotional and economic event of an older person's life is the death of a spouse. If you are married, it is completely inevitable. The adjustment and grieving period that comes in the days following the loss can be lonely and painful. As the survivor adjusts to his or her new lifestyle, there are also financial realities that must be faced. The most important advice I can give is to not make any major decisions for at least a year. Don't sell the house or move in with the kids. Let the grieving period be well underway before you make any major decision. The best way to insulate against ill-advised decisions is to have a plan in place and execute that with the help of your attorneys and financial planner.

Economically there can be huge changes in income. The monthly Social Security benefit will automatically be adjusted and it happens very quickly within 30 days of the death. The lesser of the two Social Security Benefits will be lost. If it was the primary breadwinner who died, this can mean the reduction of benefits of up to 1/3. Also, depending on the elections which were made in happier days, there may be reduced pension benefits. The death of a spouse is a time to re-evaluate your wealth strategies to make sure that all income gaps are closed. In addition, it is also time to look for new income drains and plug the holes.

The Private Pension Fund that is designed for a vast majority of our clients is intended to fill the income gap that is normally created when a spouse dies. It's hard enough emotionally to face the loss of your lifetime partner, but to afterward face a dramatically reduced income can be devastating.

With the establishment of a fund that the widowed spouse can "turn on" after the death of the partner, in most cases we see, there is no interruption of income. Those who receive payments from annuities and private pension plans generally won't lose income since almost all annuities are two-life annuities that are calculated to pay a constant amount until the death of the second annuitant.

Widows – the Largest Group of the Newly Impoverished

Almost worldwide, widows comprise a significant proportion of all women, ranging from 7% to 16% of all adult women (UN Division for the Advancement of Women, 2000). However, in some countries and regions, their proportion is far higher. In developed countries, primarily elderly women experience widowhood.

Women are more likely than men to be widowed for two reasons. First, women live longer than men (a fact highlighted by worldwide data regarding differences in life expectancies of men and women). In addition, women tend to marry older men, although this gap has been narrowing. Because women live longer and marry older men, their odds of being widowed are much greater than men's (Lee, 2002).

Loss of spouse is one of the most negative life events, next only to the loss of a child (Bennett *et al.*, 2005). Ironically, the disorganization and trauma that follow the death of a spouse seem to be greater in women than in men whenever either loses their spouse (Fasoranti *et al.*, 2007).

The largest group of the newly impoverished is widowed women. According to studies by the Social Security Administration, widowhood still remains an important risk factor for transition into poverty according to a recent report from Purvi Sevak** commissioned by the Social Security Administration.

Despite increased labor force participation rates among women and reforms under the Employee Retirement Income Security Act, widowhood remains an important risk factor for transition into poverty, although somewhat less so than 20 years ago. Women widowed at younger ages are at greatest risk for economic hardship after widowhood, and their situation declines with the duration of widowhood. We also find that women in households that are least prepared financially for widowhood are at greatest risk of a husband's death, because of the strong relationship between mortality and wealth.

*** Purvi Sevak is an Assistant Professor of Economics in the Department of Economics, Hunter College, City University of New York; David R. Weir is Research Professor and Associate Director of the Survey Research Center of the Institute for Social Research and Assistant Director of the Health and Retirement Study at the University of Michigan; and Robert J. Willis is Professor of Economics and Research Professor in the Survey Research Center and the Population Studies Center of the Institute for Social Research and the Principal Investigator for the Health and Retirement Study at the University of Michigan.*

Planning, and making sure your spouse knows the plan, are the most important parts of making the death of a spouse less traumatic.

By utilizing Accelerated Wealth Advisors' 5 Basket Strategy we can prepare for the worst while hoping for the best.

Bob and Angie: Accelerated Wealth Advisors in action:
The second D: Diagnostic

Bob and Angie both had big smiles when I greeted them. Their obvious nervousness in our first meeting was now gone. We shared a few minutes of small talk then began to go over their Social Security Maximization Report.

They were amazed by the difference in this scenario. Because they do not NEED the Social Security Benefit at retirement (we had begun a spreadsheet to work with them and show how to fill the income gap once they retired and would work with them later in the meeting on this) this strategy would optimize their benefits by an additional $306,315 if they both lived to their expected lifespan.

The seemed grateful for this information, and we continued. Bob told a tale he hadn't shared in the first meeting. As the story unfolded, I recognized it as an all too familiar tune. The tale was about Bob's brother, John. Years ago Bernie, their cousin, recommended John and his wife Mary roll their 401(k) to a Target Date Fund seven years before their planned retirement in 2012. A target date fund (TDF) is a collective investment scheme, often a mutual fund or a collective trust fund, designed to provide a simple investment solution through a portfolio whose asset allocation mix becomes more conservative as the target date approaches.

Target date funds are aimed at people planning for retirement. They have appeal because they offer a lifelong managed investment strategy and so should remain appropriate to an investor's risk profile even if left accidentally un-reviewed. Research suggests that age is by far the most important determinant in setting an investment strategy. Thus, Target Date, or age-based, funds are particularly attractive as default investment funds. They do not offer a guaranteed return but offer a convenient multi-asset retirement savings strategy through a single outcome-oriented fund.[5]

John and Mary had chosen three Target Date Funds to make sure they were protected and to accomplish what they believed was diversification.

They could not have been more wrong.

The financial meltdown of 2008 was a rough year in the market. The Dow Jones Average lost 52.3%. All of the traditional inverse relationships that existed between stocks and bonds were proven not to be accurate and those who had protested that the market correction of 2001-2002 was an anomaly were puzzled. The traditional approach of the Capital Asset Pricing Model (CAPM) to predict return and minimize risk did not work. Not only did the securities markets sink, but the value of bonds, thought to be a safe haven during a financial storm, hit bottom too. In a very short time many investors lost half of their savings. The dollars they had so carefully saved and sacrificed to have for their retirement to supplement their pensions and Social Security would now only produce half of what they had planned.

The story made my stomach turn. It's my goal in life to keep every client from experiencing that fate. That is why Accelerated Wealth Advisors use The Market Protector (MP) as an actively managed account that does not use mutual funds or individual stocks. At Accelerated Wealth we have our own in-house funds manager who is one of the brightest minds in the business. I explained to Angie and Bob how the MP account worked, especially its most critical benefit, what we call 'the essence of investment management, the management of risks, not the management of returns,' and how this worked in the 5 Basket Strategy. The MP account could reduce the risk associated with the buy and hold strategy they were used to. I could see that the level of skepticism the couple had when we first meet several weeks ago now shifted into genuine interest. As an educator, Bob really wanted to know about how all of the strategies we had showed him worked and this was no exception. Because the MP uses a data-driven approach rather than projections or predictions, the last 15 years have seen much greater gains than a mutual fund or stock account.

I turned again to Bob and Angie's statements and began to show them why Accelerated Wealth Advisors was so different. We covered retirement killers and I was able to warn them of other risks besides market corrections that needed to be anticipated. We discussed each of them. At the end of this meeting, they clearly felt more secure than they had in years.

We now entered into the Design phase where we would utilize tools to plan ahead for protection and growth.

Section IV: The Design Phase

Chapter 11

The Five Basket Strategy™

The Five Basket Strategy is designed to seek growth in any market condition while managing downside risk. Each strategy is designed to meet the individual needs of the client based on their life stage. The old saying, don't put all your eggs in one basket is particularly true when it comes to investing. The "Five Baskets of Wealth" strategy creates true diversification through a blend of non-correlated investments, which will protect and grow your wealth and insulate you from the Retirement Killers.

Each of the five baskets serves a unique purpose:

1. Income Basket – This basket holds your "I know so" money. This is your green money. These are your guaranteed payments such as Social Security and your Pension. We often will relocate some of your at-risk money to this basket, creating a Private Pension Fund.

2. Investment Basket – This basket holds your "I hope so" money. This is your red money. This money comes from your investments. After your individual strategy is in place, this basket's gains or losses will not affect the other baskets.

3. Cash Reverse Basket – This basket holds your ready money. This basket looks different for everyone. It is the amount of money on hand that you need ready access to in order to feel comfortable. Sometimes this is psychological and can be solved with many powerful strategies.

4. Long-Term Care Basket – This basket is designed to hold a reserve fund for your long-term care needs. We often leverage and relocate a portion of your assets to fill this basket. We want to create a force field around this basket as the need for long-term care can catastrophically impact your retirement if correct planning is not in place before the need arises.

5. Legacy Basket – After you and your spouse have passed away, your assets pass from the first four baskets into your legacy basket for distribution to your beneficiaries. We work to make sure the maximum efficiency and location of your other assets can mitigate the sometimes enormous tax implications to your beneficiaries upon your passing.

Everyone's baskets look different based upon their own dreams and aspirations.

Chapter 12

Creating your Private Pension Fund

Traditionally, annuities have been a popular choice for investors who want to receive a steady income stream in retirement to augment their Social Security and pension benefits. You purchase the annuity, and it then makes payments to you either immediately or at a future time. The payments can be monthly, quarterly, annually or even in a lump sum. Several factors determine how much your payments will be. Think of it as your own Private Pension Fund.

The Basics of Annuities

1. The type of annuity
   a. SPIA – Single Premium Immediate Annuity - These are safe annuities with guaranteed payments that begin as soon as, or shortly after, you sign the contract and make the single premium. They offer a guaranteed yearly payment with a low interest rate of return. They are generally utilized for Medicaid planning.

   b. Fixed annuity – A safe and guaranteed solution that can produce a period certain or lifetime income. It has a low (1-3%) interest rate and the principle will never be reduced unless you take income from it.

   c. Variable annuity – An annuity fund with a life insurance wrapper. It may have riders which guarantee a death benefit or an income stream. It is subject to market swings and has high fees (3%-5%).

   d. Fixed index – Sometimes called a hybrid, it has all of the guarantees of a fixed annuity. But because it's only linked to—not invested in—the market, it can replicate gains in the market without any of the possibilities of losses. In other words, it locks in gains and locks out losses. It can produce a lifetime income which you can never outlive and which in some cases can increase on an annual basis. Another strength and unique benefit is called "annual reset." Annual reset means that any gains the annuity experienced during that contract year are locked in and cannot ever be lost. During a down year, this annuity can never lose value.

When you will start to receive payments:

e. Under a <u>deferred annuity</u>, your money is invested for a period of time until you are ready to begin taking withdrawals, typically in retirement. During the deferral period, earnings are retained which lead to higher payments later. When the owner elects to begin receiving benefits, the deferred annuity is converted into an immediate annuity.

f. With an <u>immediate</u> annuity, you begin to receive payments soon after you make your initial investment.

How long you receive benefits:

g. <u>Income for guaranteed period</u>: You are guaranteed a specific payment amount for a set period of time (say, five years or thirty years). If you die before the end of the period, your beneficiary will receive the remainder of the payments for the guaranteed period.

h. <u>Lifetime payments</u>: A guaranteed income payout during your lifetime only; there is no survivor benefit. The payouts can be fixed or variable. The amount of the payout is determined by how much you invest and by your life expectancy. At the time of death, all payments stop - your heirs don't get anything.

i. Income for life with a guaranteed period certain benefit: A combination of a life annuity and a period certain annuity. You receive a guaranteed payout for life that includes a period certain phase. If you die during the period certain phase of the account, your beneficiary will continue to receive the payment for the remainder of the period. For example, life with a 10-year period certain is a common arrangement. If you die five years after you begin collecting, the payments continue to your survivor for five more years.

j. Joint and survivor annuity: Your beneficiary will continue to receive payouts for the rest of his or her life after you die. This is a popular option for married couples.

The money you invest in an annuity grows tax-deferred. When you eventually make withdrawals, the amount you contributed to the annuity is not taxed. The earnings are taxed at your regular income tax rate. One of the biggest advantages of annuities is that they allow you to sock away a larger amount of cash and defer paying taxes. Unlike other tax-deferred retirement accounts such as 401(k)s and IRAs, there is no annual contribution limit for an annuity. That allows you to put away more money for retirement, and is particularly useful for those that are closest to retirement age and need to catch up. If you make withdrawals before you reach age 59 ½, you will be required to pay Uncle Sam a 10% early withdrawal penalty as well as regular income tax on your investment earnings. A common misunderstanding about fixed index annuities is that if you should die before you have withdrawn the lifetime payments, the balance on the account goes to the insurance company. The annuities that Accelerated Wealth Advisors recommend forward any balance left to your beneficiaries.

Why Annuities Have Received a Black Eye

Annuities were once a staple in the toolbox of the broker/dealers. Clients understood the concept and trusted in annuities. Somewhere along the way, that changed. The reason it changed is fairly simple.

Broker/dealers sell products that may not be in your best interest. Many large investment firms put pressure on their broker/dealers to sell clients products which have high fees. Companies keep adding additional fees and surrender costs to contracts. Some companies have early surrender charges as high as 20%. Often the fees and charges are hidden in the fine print. Clients feel betrayed by the broker/dealer. In a down market, it's nearly impossible for these annuities to grow, must less maintain, their original value. These hidden fees are charged annually and often the only party making money from the variable annuity is the broker/dealer.

A fixed index has fees that range from 0%-1.25%. Before you invest, check the insurer's credit rating, a grade given by credit bureaus such as A.M. Best, Standard & Poor's and Moody's, that expresses the company's financial health. Each rating firm has its own grading scale. As a general rule, limit your options to insurers that receive either an A+ from A.M. Best or AA- or better from Moody's and S&P. You can find the ratings online, or get them from your insurance agent.

While a variable annuity has no guarantees and is subject to market adjustments, a fixed index annuity is guaranteed several ways. The insurance commissioner in each state is a member of NAIC (Nation Association of Insurance Commissioners). The insurance commissioner regulates companies that do insurance business in that state. Each company must prove on a regular basis that their solvency ratio (the amount of cash reserve they have for each insurer) is a 1:1 ratio. In other words, they must have one dollar on hand for every dollar insured. If they fall below that ratio they must recapitalize or be forced to no longer operate in that state. Their assets and liabilities will be divided proportionally among all of the other insurance companies in that state. Additionally, there are state guarantee funds that protect annuity owners if an insurance company fails. However, the coverage varies from state to state.

What Type of Annuity Is Right for Me?

During the design phase, Accelerated Wealth Advisors will help you determine what kind of an annuity should be part of your overall wealth strategy.

Chapter 13

The Infinite Bank – The 7702 Account

There is a little known financial strategy which will enable you to self-finance major purchases while growing a solid financial asset base from which you can borrow and act as your own lender. This strategy is not commonly understood. Properly structured, though, it can act as a supercharged ROTH and can create a significant tax advantage payout in your retirement. It offers tax advantages and pays dividends to you. The dividends accumulate tax-deferred until you use them in the future. Instead of carrying substantial consumer debt, you can be in debt to yourself. You can finance major consumer purchases such as education, motor vehicles, and recreational vehicles.

You can also use this strategy to self-finance real estate investments or property improvements. It's an excellent tool to use when you must take RMD's (required minimum distribution) to prevent double taxation. At Accelerated Wealth Advisors we are experts at utilizing these advanced strategies

What is this new financial vehicle that offers so many important benefits? It is actually not new at all, but it is seldom used. In addition, it's not for everybody, though it's probably a good financial solution for many people that are currently unaware of it. This proposition is likely to work well for you the more you finance consumer goods or carry consumer debt. It works for almost anyone, and it works well. If you are a small business owner, it can be an incredible way to take advantage of some sizable tax breaks.

The strategy is a substantially over-funded whole life insurance policy. This is not an investment vehicle. It is a proven, safe, and guaranteed asset accumulation vehicle.

Correctly set up, such insurance plans offer some important advantages that are unobtainable anywhere else. The key is the phrase "correctly set up." This is very important. Think of it this way, you are at a casino. You came in with $1,000. You now have $1,500 in front of you. A smart gambler takes the $500 off the table. With this strategy we are taking some of your investment winnings off the table to create your own private bank. We are also making your life insurance into your living insurance.

1. **Dividend Payments** – While they are not guaranteed, these plans have historically paid out dividends (6%-8%) which are added to the cash value of the policy. Payouts occur even in years when the stock market as a whole does poorly. Your policy is contractually bound to increase a certain amount each year. Once the dividends are paid, they are permanently added to your asset base and cannot be taken away.

2. **Tax-Deferred Growth and other Tax Advantages** – A portion of the annual premium that you pay (about half) **will** grow and create cash value in your policy. Each year the company, which is a mutual insurance company (owned by the policy holders NOT stock holders), pays a dividend to the shareholders (YOU the policy holder). That dividend has averaged 6%-8% yearly for the last 100 years. The dividend adds to the cash value of the policy and grows without being taxed and can be taken out as a loan tax-free.

3. **Guaranteed Asset Growth** – This policy can be utilized in two powerful ways. The first is for accumulating a financial asset to be used in making purchases you would have otherwise financed with credit cards or consumer loans. In addition, one of the most powerful uses of this money is leveraging it for investment growth. Second, it can be used as tax-free income in retirement.

4. **Receive Dividends on the Full Amount** – This is so important that I mention it twice. When dividends are paid, you receive dividends on the full amount of the

policy, even if you've borrowed a substantial amount to use for investments or other purposes.

5. **Consistent Growth at Very Low Risk -** Unlike the market, you'll receive consistent growth of your asset. This is very important if the primary reason you are creating this policy is to use as a private bank or credit reserve. With your money in the market, you may need it during a down period. That's the wrong time to withdraw your funds, no matter how badly you may need them. With the market, the high return funds tend to have higher associated risks. This strategy allows you to have your private bank and cash reserve with very little risk, and it is not affected by market volatility.

6. **No Age Limitations –** Maybe you'd like to retire before you reach age 59 1/2. If so, you may not touch your IRA unless you want to take a major tax penalty. You can also begin withdrawing from the policy after 70 if you have been in a financial position to wait without suffering the consequences of Required Minimum Distributions.

7. **High Liquidity –** The assets in the policy are easy to get to. You can tap them virtually at will when you need them.

8. **Reliability and Endurance –** Accelerated Wealth Advisors will assist you in choosing a company that will provide you with reliabilities and guarantees. A correctly chosen company will provide you with incredible reliability and solidity. The right insurance company will have provided unwavering growth for many decades, in some cases for

more than a century. This is obviously of the utmost importance in a banking and personal financial reserve system.

First, some of the benefits:
There are some powerful arguments for using these policies as one of the financial instruments in your arsenal. You also avoid all the problems associated with borrowing against your 401K, something you should think long and hard about before you try to do so. To effectively use an insurance policy as a financial vehicle, you must make sure the policy is correctly set up in order to maximize the advantages. Here are some of the key points.

A.   Use Only "Non-Direct Recognition" Insurance Companies. Failure to do so can result in being penalized by the insurance company for taking loans against the cash value on your policy. That goes against the reason for pursuing this strategy in the first place.

B.   The Death Benefit is Secondary. This is important. This policy is to be used while you are alive for purposes here and now.   You need to structure this policy to be substantially over-funded. You pay in to maximize the cash value while minimizing the death benefit.

C. Maximize the Cash Value with a Paid Up Premium Additions Rider. This also known as a PUP or OPP, depending upon the insurance firm. This rider gives you the option to pay into the policy in order to increase the death benefit and cash value. The money paid in not only increases the cash value. It also increases the dividends paid to you. As with the other monies, the cash value accumulates tax-deferred.

D. Don't Surrender the Policy or You Will Owe Taxes. You want to borrow against the policy, not cash it out. If you do so, you will owe the government taxes.

E. The Policy Must Pay Dividends. That's vital to using this type of vehicle successfully. If you are not using a dividend-paying whole life insurance company, this money system won't work. Dividend-paying policies are also known as "participating." This indicates you are participating in the overall earnings of the company and are thus entitled to dividends based in some way upon the profit. The dividend payments that come in, whether you have borrowed against the policy or not, are one of the keys to success when using this type of financial vehicle.

F. Use an Insurance Agent with Experience in This Specific Type of Policy. Remember, these are advanced strategies and the vast majority of agents are not familiar with them nor do they understand how to correctly set up a policy to maximize their financial benefits. At Accelerated Wealth Advisors we often use this advanced strategy to create what we call the "Rich man's ROTH." Contributions, annual premiums, can almost be unlimited unlike the restrictions the IRS places on ROTHs. This is a powerful way to repurpose and reposition income to be tax-free in retirement.

Chapter 14

The Importance of an Open HELOC

For most people, making the final mortgage payment on their home represents one of the happiest moments of their lives and proudest accomplishments. When a mortgage is created, it typically represents a 30-year obligation. Additional needs during those 30 years may necessitate a refinance, making the 30 years even longer. When you think about it, it only takes 18 years to raise an infant to adulthood!

If you have enjoyed the excitement that comes with satisfying a mortgage, the next piece of advice may sound counter-intuitive. You should remortgage your house by creating a Home Equity Line of Credit. A Home Equity Line of Credit (often called HELOC) is a loan which allows you to borrow against the equity in your home. It is secured against your home, so it is mortgage. However, you don't pay any interest unless and until you borrow money from the line of credit. Most lenders will give you a checkbook and the ability to transfer funds online for instant access to your money. If you do borrow, the interest is tax-deductible on Schedule A of your income tax return.

For individuals with paid-off homes and reasonable credit ratings, the fees associated with the creation of a HELOC tend to be minimal. You are the type of client the bank wants – one who really doesn't need to borrow the bank's money. The timing regarding the creation of this loan is crucial. You want to create this loan while you and/or your spouse are still working. Under the post real estate crash regulations, your banker will need to see that you have income in order to offer you a traditional HELOC.

Creating the HELOC is crucial even if you don't have a present need for the money. The interest rate on a HELOC loan is always going to be less than any unsecured debt. The HELOC creates a safety net for unseen expenses that would otherwise be placed on a credit card at a higher interest rate. It also creates an opportunity fund of cash which may allow you to take advantage of unexpected occasions like a last- minute 50% off deal on your dream vacation. Also, if you have high-interest debt of any kind, you can easily plug that wealth drain by transferring the debt to the lower interest, tax-deductible HELOC.

Chapter 15

Market Protection: Maximizing your Return and Controlling Risk

Warren Buffet – "2 rules of investment:
1. Don't lose money
2. Don't forget rule number 1"

Benjamin Graham, the "Dean of Wall Street," says: "The essence of investment management is the management of risk, not the management of returns."

Traditionally, there have been three primary philosophies of investing:

1. **Prediction-Based Investing** – The Prediction Model of investment is an approach involving <u>statistical inference</u>. The emphasis is on the prediction of future economic events based on past observations. This is the equivalent of driving while looking in the rearview mirror.

2. **Theory-Based Investing** – There are several academic theories of investing:
    - Efficient Markets Hypothesis
    - Rational Investor Theory
    - Modern Portfolio Theory
    - Efficient Frontier
    - Strategic Asset Allocation (pie charts)

    Many of these academic theories have been around a long time. They make sense on paper, but fail to perform in the real world as promised. Traditional asset allocation says to diversify in order to protect from volatility and loss, but many portfolios are heavily vested in various types of equities. In bear markets, diversification falls short.

3. **Data-Driven Approach** – At Accelerated Wealth Advisors this is the strategy we utilize to manage risk and maximize returns. The data-driven model involves analyzing current data and trends to make investment decisions based on short and long-term signals, which

the market generates. By using this approach our clients participate in the gains and not the losses of the market. This is in contrast to the "buy and hold" strategy of many broker/ dealers.

Traditional investment theory says that higher returns are only possible if risk is increased. Advisors position clients in portfolios designed for them to experience the maximum risk they  say they can tolerate in order to obtain desired returns. We believe this approach to risk and reward is flawed since it is based on passive asset management. Clients ideally want higher returns with limited risk. Government intervention into markets has created a continued cycle of boom and bust. We must have a strategy that participates in booms and protects in busts. We believe this is possible with active strategies.

At Accelerated Wealth Advisors, we believe there is a better way – Active Management. We use a data-driven model which listens to the markets and reacts rather than trying to make predictions or using academic theories that only work in the classroom. By data evaluation, we know markets go through long periods of trending. We identify these trends and participate in the uptrends, and protect against the down trends.

Active management can be described very simply. While boating, when faced with the choice of rowing or sailing, the proper answer depends on the environment. If there is a wind, sail. If there is no wind, row. Investing is the same. You choose a strategy based upon the environment. As a country, we remain in a long-term bear market. This means the prudent strategy is to row. By actively managing the portfolio we are able to participate in the short-term bull markets, and protect during the bear market.

Building an Investment Strategy
Our strategy is simple. We want to build an investment strategy that satisfies all of the criteria below.

- ✓ Belief-based
- ✓ All-season approach
- ✓ Safety first
- ✓ Proven
- ✓ Minimize pain
- ✓ Data driven
- ✓ Systematic

Chapter 16

Secure Estate and Legacy Planning

Estate Planning

The dictionary defines a legacy as an amount of money or property left to someone under a will, but it is actually so much more. A legacy is also family history, wisdom, and traditions you pass on to future generations. Warren Buffett said, "I want to leave my children enough that they can do anything, but not so much that they can do nothing." You are the steward of your legacy, which has both monetary assets and intangible assets. Eventually this role will be taken on by the members of future generations. Leaving your money to your children is a great accomplishment, but you want to do it in a way that helps them and doesn't harm them. To accomplish that goal, you need to create an estate plan that addresses the individual issues of your family.

At a minimum, an estate plan should consist of three documents:

- Financial power of attorney
- Medical power of attorney
- Basic will

A financial power of attorney gives another person, your agent, the authority to act on your behalf. Unless the power of attorney is limited, your agent can enter into any agreement or complete any transaction, which you can legally do.

A financial power of attorney may be immediate. This allows your agent to act on your behalf at any time until the document is revoked. The other option is to have the financial power of attorney become active only if you are certified as being unable to make and/or communicate decisions on your own behalf. This is known as a springing power of attorney.

The second document is a medical power of attorney. This allows your agent to consult with your doctors and make medical decisions on your behalf if you are unable to do so. Rest assured, your doctors will attempt to get you to consent to your decisions as long as you are at least marginally confident to do so. Medical powers of attorney also usually contain an "Advanced Medical Directive." Most people refer to this more simply as a Living Will. It is a set of instructions by you. It states what treatments you want or don't want in the event further treatment serves no medically reasonable chance of curing you.

The third document contained in a basic estate plan is a Last Will and Testament. Under this document you appoint an individual, a team of individuals, or an institution to handle your affairs after you are deceased. The people or institutions appointed to do this are known as the executor or personal representative depending on where you live. The executor is put in charge of gathering your assets (also called marshaling), having them valued, liquidating your assets, paying your bills including any estate taxes, and distributing the proceeds to your beneficiaries either outright or in trust, as you have directed.

If you don't have a will, your assets will pass as governed by the intestate laws of succession of the state in which you live. The word "intestate" means that you have died without a valid will. The law of intestacy sets forth who is entitled to what under your estate. The court, rather than a personal representative or executor, appoints an administrator. The administrator can be any family member, friend or institution. In most states, preference is given to the next of kin if there are multiple people seeking appointment. The administrator carries out the same duties as the executor. In most states, the processes, costs and taxes associated with intestate succession are the exact same as if you had died with a will. The law sets forth who is to receive what of your property. All states are different but basically most intestate laws read as follows:

Assets pass to:
1.   The spouse. If there is no living spouse…
2.   The children. If there are no living children…
3.   The parents of the deceased. If no living parent…
4.   The siblings of the deceased. If no living siblings…
5.   The aunts and uncles of the deceased. If non-living…
6.   The first cousins of the deceased. If nonliving…
7.   Other biological relations in order of their direct relationship to the deceased.

Eventually, if nobody can be identified that is eligible to receive, the estate escheats to the state in which you live. To "escheat" means the money is paid to the state. Most states have designated what agency within the state receives the funds. For instance, many laws read that the money goes to the school district in which you resided before you died.

While you should have a basic estate plan at a bare minimum, you may want to consider going further. Trust- based planning gives you more options and control. If one of your children has special needs and is entitled to receive governmental benefits because of those needs, a Special Needs Trust is almost mandatory. This allows you to give funds to the special needs child without endangering his or her governmental benefits.

If you have a "problem child," you may also want to consider special needs planning. The term "problem child" can be defined many different ways. It is not a legal term of art. This is the adult child who in some ways never grew up. This is the child who, if given large sums of money at one time, will harm himself or herself. A problem child could have many issues that make giving money to him or her directly a bad idea. To name a few: drug addiction, alcoholism, and inability to manage money, gambling issues or a child in an unstable marriage. By creating a trust, you name a trustee to be the steward of the inheritance of the problem child. You can create the terms under which money is released to the problem child. These instructions will then be followed after your death.

You may also want to consider creating a trust if there are no problem, only successful, children. Occasionally, the next generation does not need all of your wealth because they have done well on their own. If this is the case,  you may want to create a multigenerational trust that preserves wealth for the needs of future generations. One of the biggest benefits of this type of trust is a tax savings. When you pass money directly to your children, there will be inheritance taxes levied. If they don't need the funds, they are likely to invest the funds, which hopefully will grow. When your child dies, both the asset and the growth are taxed in his or her estate. By creating a multigenerational tax, you have the ability to avoid the additional layer of taxation. There are tax rules as to how much money can pass this way, but in general it is a win. There are also many other ways trusts can be used for tax planning and tax savings. These techniques are often referred to as the alphabet soup of estate planning because of the acronyms given to many of the trusts:

Grantor Retained Annuity Trust – GRAT
Grantor Retained Investment Trust - GRIT
Charitable Remainder Uni-Trust – CRUT
Charitable Lead Trust - CLT
Irrevocable Life Insurance Trust – ILIT
Revocable Living Trust – RLT

Your estate plan can also be a wonderful way to leave gifts to your favorite charities. A word of caution, do your homework. Find out how bequests are used by the organization you are considering. Are you giving it to a local charity or a national charity? Where does your money actually go? If you don't restrict it, how will it be used? Many organizations treat unrestricted gifts as a general legacy and use them for general day-to-day operations. If that is what you don't want, be specific as to which program or programs the gift can be used to support. If you want the gift to go to a restricted endowment, you must be specific. Under a restricted endowment the organization can use only the income generated by the gift. Also, if your charity is part of a national or international organization and you wish your money to be used locally be very specific. This is especially true with organizations such as the Catholic Church where governance is done on a regional level. If you want the gift to stay at your parish, you must indicate that in writing.

Gifting
Another powerful legacy planning tool is gifting assets away to individuals and organizations during your lifetime. Under the Internal Revenue Code, currently you can gift up to $14,000 per individual per year without triggering the need to file a gift tax return. You can gift over this amount, but are required to file a gift tax return. Generally, you don't actually pay gift tax on amounts over $14,000; the amount due is deducted from your Federal Estate Tax Credit.

If, after a complete analysis of an individual's assets and needs, it is obvious that they have far more wealth than they could ever spend, a gifting plan should be devised to get the excess wealth out of his or her estate. If the excess assets aren't gifted, both the value of the asset and the growth will be included in the estate and subject to federal and state inheritance tax. In the appendix you will find a current table of state level inheritance and death tax rates. Systematic gifting can eliminate much of this problem.

Gifts can either be given outright to your children or placed in trust. One often-overlooked tool is to purchase whole life insurance for the child or grandchildren. This can create infinite banks for many future generations while creating a huge tax savings. Also, lifetime gifting to charities is an excellent use of excess assets. Within most investors' portfolios are gifts that have high capital gains. These are investments which have done incredibly well. The problem is that the sale of this investment can trigger high capital gains taxes. If the asset is gifted to your favorite charity, it can be sold by the charity, which is exempt from capital gains taxes. Also, many individuals who are charitably inclined donate their annual required minimum distribution to the charity of their choice thus avoiding income taxes on the gift.

The Taxman Cometh

The only thing as certain as death is taxes. This is particularly true when death and taxes collide. Death triggers a chain reaction of taxable events. These consequences result both at the federal and state level.

Federal Taxes

If your estate was worth less than $5,340,000.00 you are exempt from the payment of federal inheritance taxes. Estate tax exemptions change, so you will want to confirm with your adviser. The executor or personal representative of estates over this amount are required to file an inheritance tax return within 9 months of death and pay inheritances taxes. See the chart in the appendix for the current rates. A word about the federal inheritance tax exemption amount: it is a political football and subject to change. As the federal debt grows and congress feels more pressure, there have been discussions of reducing this amount, which would make more estates subject to the "death tax." It is crucial to have an advisor on the team monitoring your assets and the federal exemption amount.

Even if you escape the federal inheritance tax, there are still federal tax consequences triggered by death. Your final income tax return must be filed. Also, depending on how long your estate remains open, your executor may need to file fiduciary income tax returns. The good news, all non-qualified assets held in your estate get a step-up in basis at the time of your death. On assets with high built-in capital gains, this can be of incredible value to the heirs. Rather than your vacation home being worth the $10,000 you paid for it, it is worth its current $1 million value as of the date of your death. This means a huge savings on capital gains tax if the heirs elect to sell.

Remember the tax time bombs we discussed earlier? If they have not already been defused or exploded, here is where they detonate. If your 401K, IRA, or SEP is part of your estate, there will be tax issues for your heirs. The asset will be included in your estate for federal inheritance tax purposes. Note: some states exclude this value of qualified assets, bypassing a beneficiary designation.

Your beneficiary will be required to make an election as to how they wish to receive the funds. The two basic options are lump sum distribution or distribution over five years. Beneficiaries who elect for lump sum distribution will take a huge tax hit in the year that the asset is distributed. Not only do they have to pay the deferred tax, but this will most likely put them into a higher tax bracket which in turn leads to paying more taxes. Taking the money out over five years usually results in the payment of fewer taxes because it is less likely that the beneficiary will land in a different tax bracket. There is also the ability to enter into a stretch-out IRA, this allows for the recalculation of the life expectancy based in part upon the age of the beneficiary. This will allow the money to remain tax-deferred longer, but arguably the asset just becomes a time bomb in the estate of the beneficiary.

If the tax time bomb has already been defused as suggested in previous chapters, the heirs will be in a much better tax position. If the qualified asset was relocated to an annuity, the beneficiary of that annuity has greater flexibility regarding payment options. In many instances they can re-purpose the annuity to meet his or her income needs.

If the qualified asset was relocated to a whole life policy, the proceeds of the policy can be used to help defer any estate taxes. Furthermore, if someone other than the deceased owned the whole life policy, the proceeds are not included in the calculation of the taxable estate for estate tax purposes.

State Level Taxes

Estates are also taxed at the state level. There are basically two different approaches states take when it comes to inheritance taxes. One approach is direct taxation of the estate. If you die in a state which uses this approach, your executor or personal representative will file a separate state inheritance tax return. Different states have different definitions of what makes up your gross estate. For instance, some states do not include assets that passed under your beneficiary designations (life insurance, qualified plans, and assets with a TOD — Transfer on Death — designation or POD -Payable on Death — designation).

The second approach is not to have a separate state death tax, but to have a piggyback tax. If a state has a piggyback tax law in place, basically they will collect part of what gets paid to the Federal government if the estate was federally taxable. If states have a direct death tax, it is deductible on the federal inheritance tax return. States with piggyback taxes are basically getting the money that would have been the deduction.

Your executor will also be responsible for filing your state and local income tax returns. Depending on how long the estate remains open, there may also be the need to file fiduciary income tax returns if the estate has income.

Bob and Angie: Accelerated Wealth Advisors in action:
The third D: Design

Bob and Angie walked into the office for their third visit to be greeted with coffee, just the way they liked it, and a freshly baked cookie. They had been blown away by the attention they had received through this process.   Bob had more questions about Social Security and they had been expertly answered with a phone call to the office.   Bob's office was changing and when he had questions about taxes and tax-favored positions, a forensic accountant available via a quick phone conference who thoroughly explained why relocating some of their nest egg into a life insurance basket would result in some long-term tax advantages.

Bob liked that Wealth Advisors were thorough and knowledgeable on so many aspects of retirement planning. And, there always seemed to be an expert on any subject or strategy available to him when he needed them.   That's what we call the "Integrated Resource Network." Bob's initial reaction when I first mentioned this was, "yeah, sure, part of a sales pitch." Now he was beginning to see it was nothing of the kind. Accelerated Wealth Advisors' mission was to provide the best education and resources to each client.

I gathered up the file for Bob and Angie and moved toward the conference room. I could tell Bob was chewing on another big question. We had discussed Long Term Care at the last meeting and now Bob wanted to know what the plan was.

Bob and Angie had avoided this issue like many baby boomers. They were healthy and in the perfect plan they would never need any. Angie, who had spent a career in nursing, jumped in. "Well, I have seen the disaster an unexpected illness can bring to a family both in heartache and financially. I have seen the stress on their faces when faced with rehab and a possible nursing home. None of us want this and I guess Bob and I have been in denial about it. We have just hoped that we would both be healthy and one night we would go to bed and BOTH of us would not wake up the next morning! We know that's not realistic and we have both been afraid and looking forward to this part of our education."

I glanced over the file. "You both have some long-term care insurance. What do you like most about it?"

"Well, we like that we have $100 a day if we have to go into a nursing home," she said.

Bob jumped into the conversation. "But we are worried that on a retirement income, if they keep raising premiums, will we be able to afford it?"

I added, "And what if you never need it? You could always self-insure, but a 3-5 year nursing home stay could deplete all you have saved and change the retirement for the surviving spouse dramatically. No one wants to move in with the kids."

I took them through the 5 Basket Strategy. This strategy works not by simply allocating a part of your retirement fund, but by relocating a portion from a position of risk into a no-risk solution that will not only provide long-term care if you need it but also remain liquid for emergencies or changes in one's life. Best of all, by leveraging this part of one's nest egg by relocating from the investment basket to the long-term basket, if you never need it, it will then pass to the children tax-free!

As I began the education on this solution, both Bob and Angie were thrilled. The Five Basket Strategy planned for long-term care, taxes, social security, the death of a spouse, and an avalanche of other risks, all while minimizing fees and losses. I was able to show them how they needed to allocate some of their retirement for income and further investment, so that even when they were retired, their investments could continue to grow. This meant they could never outlive their money.

Bob, Angie, and I went through all of the baskets and worked together. It was a bittersweet meeting because I knew the next would be the last for a little while.

Section V

The 4th D: The Delivery

The Delivery portion of the plan is the best part. Here we see the puzzle come together. The pieces interlock and the strategy is now in place.

It is not static. John Lennon said, "Life is what happens when you're busy making other plans." Life changes, we change, markets change, and sometimes goals and circumstances change. At Accelerated Wealth Advisors, each wealth strategy is designed to take into consideration current needs and dreams as well as to provide for possible world events and personal changes in each of our lives. Liquidity and access to funds for any eventuality is a key part of our strategies. Making sure that whatever the next day's news may bring or whatever roadblock is thrown in front of us can be addressed is the true essence of planning. Hope for the best, but be prepared for the worst. We all hope we will never fall ill with Alzheimer's or cancer or some life-altering disease.

None of us want to spend any time in a nursing home, but some of us will. None of us want to lose our spouse early, but it happens. We hope inflation will always be under control, but we know it has been as high as 17% per year in the past. We hope for world peace, but know it has been elusive. We hope there will never be another 911 but know in this dangerous world it is a real possibility. In short, hope is not a strategy. We must plan for as many eventualities as possible and have a ship that can weather the storm, stay on course and lead us to safe waters more often than not. THAT is the difference in financial planning and wealth strategy. We live it!

At Accelerated Wealth®, our goal is to deliver a comprehensive wealth strategy plan tailored to the needs of each unique client with whom we work through a collaborative effort using an integrated wealth strategy team. We want to help you cultivate the fuel for your dreams! I hope that you have found this guide helpful, and that tonight you sleep soundly.

Bob and Angie: Accelerated Wealth Advisors in action:
The fourth D: Delivery

The Barnes returned to the office three weeks later to take delivery. The delivery meeting is my favorite because I knew Bob and Angie would be secure in their savings and retirement. I looked over their file once more to make sure everything was in order. There would be future meetings; for example, they needed a meeting with our estate attorney to implement their legacy goals for their children and grandchildren.

As I approached Bob and Angie they looked the way I want all of my clients to look: well rested and excited for the future.

54717044R10082

Made in the USA
Middletown, DE
06 December 2017